Other Books by Gretchen Oltman

The Supreme 15: Cases and Study Materials for AP Government and Politics Exam, 2019

The Themes That Bind Us: Simplifying U.S. Supreme Court Cases for the Social Studies Classroom, 2018

Law Meets Literature: A Novel Approach for the English Classroom, 2015

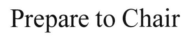

Prepare to Chair

Prepare to Chair

Leading the Dissertation and Thesis Process

Gretchen Oltman
Jeanne L. Surface
Kay Keiser

ROWMAN & LITTLEFIELD
Lanham • Boulder • New York • London

Published by Rowman & Littlefield
An imprint of The Rowman & Littlefield Publishing Group, Inc.
4501 Forbes Boulevard, Suite 200, Lanham, Maryland 20706
www.rowman.com

6 Tinworth Street, London SE11 5AL

British Library Cataloguing in Publication Information Available

Library of Congress Cataloging-in-Publication Data

Names: Oltman, Gretchen A., author. | Surface, Jeanne L., 1960– author. | Keiser, Kay A., author.
Title: Prepare to chair : leading the dissertation and thesis process / Gretchen Oltman, Jeanne L. Surface, Kay Keiser.
Description: Lanham, Maryland : Rowman & Littlefield, [2019] | Includes bibliographical references and index.
Identifiers: LCCN 2019003226 (print) | LCCN 2019011461 (ebook) | ISBN 9781475842630 (Electronic) | ISBN 9781475842616 (cloth : alk. paper) | ISBN 9781475842623 (pbk. : alk. paper)
Subjects: LCSH: Graduate students--Supervision of—United States. | Faculty advisors—United States. | Counseling in higher education—United States. | Dissertations, Academic—Authorship. | Universities and colleges—United States—Graduate work.
Classification: LCC LB2371 (ebook) | LCC LB2371 .O47 2019 (print) | DDC 808.06/6378—dc23
LC record available at https://lccn.loc.gov/2019003226

∞ ™ The paper used in this publication meets the minimum requirements of American National Standard for Information Sciences Permanence of Paper for Printed Library Materials, ANSI/NISO Z39.48-1992.

Printed in the United States of America

To our own dissertation chairs, who provided the insights, support, and expertise on our doctoral journeys and to the students we have had the privilege to mentor through this process.

Contents

Preface

Every experience has a beginning, a first attempt, setbacks, memorable events, and hopefully triumphs. So it is for becoming a dissertation or thesis Chair. This craft is not taught in a class, and it is an add-on to a very busy and ambitious career in higher education. Does anyone dream of someday becoming a Chair? Probably not, yet for all the extra effort and energy needed to shepherd candidates through their novice research, there is nothing more rewarding than being the catalyst who guides students successfully to the capstone of their degrees and the realization of their dreams.

Our own experiences as Chairs have shaped our practices and opinions about the process. All three of us work in higher education and have both earned terminal degrees and served on committees for students earning their degrees as well. Quite honestly, the process is usually trial by fire. That is, none of us were formally trained to effectively lead a thesis or dissertation committee but were assumed upon hiring that our skill set would provide adequate tools by which to do so. This was sometimes true, yet at other times, we found ourselves lacking practicality, guidance, or insights held by more experienced Chairs. By sharing our insights and personal reflections in this early section of the book, we hope that others can avoid common pitfalls so that their students are guided efficiently, effectively, and ethically from the initial brainstorming to the final publication of their thesis or dissertation.

KAY'S STORY

The summer of 2005 was both an end and a beginning for me. I attended my first dissertation defense—my own. I greatly overprepared and presented a breadth of details so that all questions would be answered before they were asked. In the end, it was a rewarding experience, and I was extremely grateful for the support of my Chair.

Then in the space of one weekend I went from being hooded as a Doctor of Education to starting as assistant professor at my alma mater. Suddenly, my professors were my peers and my students had been former classmates. I lived in fear that my limited knowledge would be discovered and was amazed that those who had known me well as a student now turned to me for wisdom and advice. Sometimes I should have asked my department peers instead of being brave and foolish. Sometimes I should have been bold and not doubted my intuition.

As a brand-new dissertation committee member, I had the unusual advantage of knowing exactly how students saw each of the faculty, what the shortcomings of the norms and procedures were, and what ideas, formats, and behaviors were prized by this group. If I had come from another university, I would have had another lens through which to view the system. At first, this insider viewpoint was a help to me. I did not have a depth of knowledge in fields or methods beyond my own, but I knew more than other faculty how the students had been taught and what their folk wisdom was. I also knew the faculty philosophies and idiosyncrasies, and this allowed me to give timely advice to struggling students.

Over time, however, this narrow experience of only one graduate program led to expectations that all programs had the same rules and requirements. What a shock it was for me to sit on a committee at another university. Unbreakable rules were merely guidelines, and everything from the paperwork to the pecking order was unfamiliar. Learning about the procedures in other departments, colleges, and universities can only strengthen the decision making for the individuals creating new research and the committees creating new researchers.

I started my career as an elementary teacher and administrator. It has been interesting to have graduate students who were in my sixth-grade classroom. In comparing the memory of the young student to the current one nearing a doctoral hood, I always notice that they have not changed all that much. Graduate students are more polished, quicker to cope, and have a more adult façade. When stressed or excited, though, the habits, strengths, and weaknesses of childhood peek out.

I am still that elementary teacher just under the surface, and I see the tender young learner in each candidate. It is easy to crush dreams through a thoughtless word or a misunderstood message. One smile or thoughtful praise can last in the student's memory long after the teacher has moved on to new students and new challenges. I believe teaching, and being a Chair, is a solemn, sacred trust that should not be taken lightly or callously. Many students have come to me in tears, with angry frustration, or with the intention of giving up, and I am proud of everyone I now call doctor.

By this time, I have chaired more than 50 dissertations and been a member on more than double that for dissertations and theses in education, arts and sciences, and fine arts. Most questions I am asked I have heard before, and yet still I learn with each new candidate and committee. If I could go back and give advice to myself in 2005, it would be to worry less, share more, and know all the relevant policies and procedures that might impact the research. I would caution myself not to make decisions that future students could use as precedents to manipulate the system. I would be transparent about my pet peeves and biases and try to mitigate them through other faculty support. Finally, I would intentionally nurture each relationship rather than relying on habit. When candidate and Chair together have finished their crafting of new research, the mentor is a peer, the student is a master, and what remains is the relationship.

GRETCHEN'S STORY

When I entered graduate school, it was almost because I had never *not* been a student. By the time I entered my PhD program, I was already a lawyer and was working as a high school English teacher. Earning my PhD kept me where I loved to be—in the halls of the university.

I can honestly admit today that I had no idea what a dissertation was when I began my graduate program. I learned what lay ahead shortly before I was to stumble into the proposal process. During my dissertation proposal meeting, I was shocked at the level of disagreement and discourse that took place between my committee members. I remember looking helplessly at my Chair as he tried to intervene and redirect the conversation, and I left the meeting in tears because it appeared that my proposal had passed, but with a list of suggestions for research options that seemed undoable to me. I left the meeting thinking I would never finish my degree and at that point, I was completely fine with that decision.

The next day, I received three letters of apology from my committee members. They assured me that their disagreements with each other were more about interoffice politics and methodology than about my proposal. To this day, I am the only person I know who has received apology letters after that meeting. Needless to say, by that point, I had given up.

I let a couple of years pass and at the insistence of my Chair, picked up the now dusty proposal and started working again. I still had the same fire for the topic. It was something that truly lived within me and not finishing it was not an option. I managed to scrape by every extended deadline offered by the university in order to graduate nearly 10 years after having started my program. My dissertation defense was a celebratory event with the same committee members, and I went on to earn a national dissertation award.

I entered the world of chairing dissertations about three years after graduation and suddenly found myself as a learner all over again. Each student who approached me with a topic left me confused, wondering how to say "No, think about it this way . . . ," and puzzled at the methods I had never employed as a student. As I write today, I have served as a Dissertation Consultant for my university (basically someone who works solely with the process of drafting, writing, and revising dissertations) and eventually as a Chair and committee member.

I wish I could say that dissertations are now easy for me to chair, but they are not. I received no formal training about our university's policies or procedures. The dissertation model in my department was under development much of the time I was there, so there was much polite disagreement among scholars as to what constitutes a "good" dissertation. It was a trial by fire, to say the least. I am an apt learner but found myself engrossed in literature on topics I had never read about before and was ordering methodology textbooks in order to somehow teach myself how to coach a student's research design.

On top of the dissertation piece itself, the complexity of working with graduate students in an online program was also difficult. My own experience had been sitting face-to-face with my Chair and visiting his office often for advice and reassurance. Online students are in a different class—they work hard but never have the convenience of showing up on campus and sitting down with their Chair whenever they feel like it. Add to this the difficulties of being a working adult, writing a dissertation, managing childcare, and having no personal connection to campus, and the anxiety level of the student was quite high. Most handled it like champions, but I could feel their stress and anxiety as defense days drew near and angry emails and nervous phone calls bombarded my office.

The one piece that I carried directly from my dissertation Chair was the necessity of patience. My Chair was an intelligent, patient scholar about 30 years my senior. He was a good listener, always encouraging, and always believed in what I could accomplish. However, he was also honest 100% of the time. Sometimes this really hurt my feelings. Writings I had pored over were soon questioned for validity and quality.

Through my years of this academic exercise, I was able to learn what a real academic mentor is. He not only challenged me, but even after I graduated, he continued to guide my career and offer insights on the current state of affairs in education. As I began working with my own dissertation students, I would often recall the amount of patience my advisor showed me and would check my own short temper or my wish that I could get something else on my to-do list done. The investment my Chair made in me continues to be something I try to model with my own students.

Writing this book is one way I hope to help someone like myself—someone who enters the university, part- or full-time, and begins working with a thesis or dissertation student with no formal training in doing so. Granted, each discipline hosts its own set of norms and customs, but having anything, something like this book to help me know when to ask questions, seek counsel from others, and simply help a student through a difficult time would have been a godsend and I hope readers find it to be so.

JEANNE'S STORY

We all three have different stories, and the one thing I will say at the very beginning of my story is that I wish I had had Kay as my dissertation Chair. I hope that her students understand how fortunate they are to be blessed with her guidance and support. I wrote my dissertation while I was serving as a school superintendent in a tiny school district in a very remote area of the country. I was overwhelmed with the supervision of ball games nearly every night.

The other responsibilities that engulfed me were accreditation, assessments, bus routes, a swimming pool that was eating up our school budget, monthly meetings with the state's school facilities commission for a major school remodel, working with a board of education for the first time, the building of the new superintendent residence, and making sure the school was well maintained and the buses were running. In addition to that, being a leader in a small community means being asked to serve as a leader for other organizations. Along with all of this, my teenage daughter was having a hard time adjusting to the new school, and her well-being was worrisome.

My university was seven hours from my home. The only sure support that I had in the process was the library and my longtime mentor, who was not at this university. I would order books and materials, and they arrived in my mailbox within four days, and that was with mail delivery every other day.

The time I spent working on my dissertation typically fell on Sunday. There were no ball games to attend and on Saturday we made the 45-minute trip to the nearest grocery store to restock for the week. The dissertation was an escape for me. I was very interested in my topic, and I was fortunate to know people across the country who were able to answer questions. My longtime mentor was the Dean of Education of the college that was 15 minutes from my first principalship. We kept in close contact, and he was always available to read my drafts via email and give me feedback and encouragement throughout the process.

My university was not as friendly as my mentor and my other colleagues. Being over seven hours from my university made it difficult for some of my coursework due to weather patterns. I lived in the mountains, and my university had a lower altitude; the land area was a mix of prairie and mountains. One of the most devastating experiences I had that still impacts my work today was missing a three-day weekend class of advanced statistics due to a major blizzard in my area of the state. I had never been a math whiz and to miss a big weekend left me lacking in some important knowledge. There was no way to make it up. My coursework was complete, and there was no further contact from my professors.

To this day, of a group of 15 of us, I believe that only six have doctorates. I was the only female of five who made it to graduation. The process of obtaining a doctoral degree was a mystery that I had to solve on my own. Fortunately, there was some interest from another professor in the department, and we decided to conduct a focus group with superintendents; I took the focus group another step and conducted case studies of the superintendents.

The whole mess was backward. I started with the interviews and focus groups, then wrote the literature review and proposal. I presented my proposal from a distance and didn't receive any feedback for over a month. I wondered if I had failed. I finally made a phone call to my dissertation Chair, and he told me that I did just fine, and I should keep writing. I wrote, sent chapters, and waited and waited. My longtime mentor told me to wait several weeks and then call. This trend continued throughout the dissertation. At one point my mentor asked me if I just wanted to give up. So, I pushed harder.

I scheduled a trip to the university to meet with my Chair. Fortunately, my Chair lived near the university and although he had forgotten our meeting he was able to meet with me after a phone call. The meeting was not especially productive, but at least he knew that I was making progress.

A blessing came in the form of a new faculty member who had not finished her dissertation. She was writing a qualitative dissertation and was able to help me finish. Finally, my defense was scheduled. My Chair suggested that I defend the week of graduation so that I didn't have to make an additional trip to the university. I took a week off and came to the university. I spent the first two days working on edits that my Chair had finally shared and on the third day I defended. The defense was hard. I presented, and the committee left for an hour. My Chair came back and explained that I would need to make some edits, but all was well. I was able to go through graduation.

After the defense, I was told that I needed to have approval from the Institutional Review Board (IRB), which was on campus, and a few other hoops to jump through. I went back to the hotel room and finished. The signature page was being passed around to the committee, and one of the members said she does not sign off on dissertations the week of graduation. I walked through the ceremony and waited for two weeks for her to sign off on the paperwork. I never understood her behavior, but I now believe that it was rooted in a conflict with my Chair rather than me.

Fast forward 15 years. I had no inkling that I would become a professor. I've come to a beautiful place in higher education and love what I do. Being a Chair has given me the opportunity to meet the needs of students in a way that I think makes the challenge of writing a dissertation more manageable to professionals with young families. At the same time, every day is an experiment for me as I realize how much I don't know. I often say that I'm "learning along the way." I can't think of a better way to describe being a dissertation Chair. Every dissertation, every student, and certainly every method or approach brings a new challenge to my work. I love being a Chair.

Now that I am in a department that is highly functional, has strong leadership, and has a system that is followed to assign dissertation Chairs and complete all of the steps required by the university in an orderly fashion, including getting permission from the institutional review board before conducting the research, I feel better about my dissertation experience. I realize that the department at my university was highly dysfunctional. Constant turnover in the department was a sign of problems that I hadn't realized at that time. I pushed my way through my program with little support from the university and tremendous responsibilities at home. I was set to fail. I made it despite the odds against me.

If I can give any advice to Chairs and committee members, it would be to create a process that sets students up for success. Know your university's expectations for graduate students and for writing dissertations. Organize and communicate a consistent process for all Chairs within your college or department for each step of the dissertation. Explain the expectations of being on a committee to members of the committee and especially to outside members. Outline the requirements for completion of the dissertation for your students, including everything from IRB approval to applying for graduation and sending in the dissertation for publication.

SOME HELPFUL DEFINITIONS FOR THIS BOOK

In order to collectively write about the thesis and dissertation process, it is helpful to have an understanding of the working definitions used in this book. While these definitions apply to the context here, the terms are widely universal to many institutions and committee structures.

Chair: The lead member of a thesis or dissertation committee. This person is sometimes referred to as an "Advisor" or "Supervisor." The Chair oversees the research process, works individually with the student throughout the research process, works with the student to manage a schedule to completion, and is responsible for managing and leading the committee.

Committee: A group of scholars assigned to advise and affirm a student's thesis or dissertation study. This group may be composed of novice or veteran faculty (or any mix thereof), professionals in the field, and/or a multidisciplinary team. Typically, committees range from three to five members, depending on institutional requirements. The committee guides the student research, advises the Chair on scholarly issues, and votes on the final status of the student.

Defense: A formal presentation in which the entire content of the dissertation is explained and presented. Generally done as an oral presentation, this committee meeting might take place virtually or face-to-face, depending on the institution's requirements. The defense is generally considered a public meeting and is a chance for the university community to learn about the student's original research. After the student's presentation, committee members may ask questions or provide feedback. Committee members then vote on whether to pass or fail the student.

Dissertation: an original, scholarly research study completed in order to earn a terminal doctoral degree. In the context of this book, the terminal degree could be a PhD or EdD, which requires a formal proposal (or prospectus) and dissertation defense in order to earn the credential. Some terminal degrees may require only coursework without a dissertation (such as an MD or JD). There is no one standard format for a dissertation and the length of a dissertation can vary widely.

Graduate Student: an individual enrolled at an institution of higher education (college or university) at the post-bachelor's level in a degree-seeking program. Graduate students may study on campus, virtually, part-time, full-time, or any combination thereof.

Proposal: A written draft (or drafts) of the thesis or dissertation that is refined according to Chair or committee feedback. Sometimes called a "Prospectus," the proposal can vary in form, but generally presents enough information for the committee to vote on the study design, overall original scholarly nature of the study, and general quality of the student's paper. A "proposal meeting" is typically held in which committee members provide feedback and vote on whether the student may conduct the study.

Thesis: A long essay or original research study written in order to earn a graduate degree. Most students completing a thesis earn a master's degree. The thesis is sometimes referred to as a "dissertation" at some institutions, but for the purposes of this book, the term will refer to the written requirement necessary to earn a master's degree.

HOW TO USE THIS BOOK

This book is intended to fill the gaps for new and experienced Chairs ("Chairs" as we will call those in this role throughout this book, although the term is different in many places—some call this role "advisor," or "supervisor") who may have never had formal training on how to be a Chair. We acknowledge that all Chairs bring with them their own experiences as a student and this may be an asset or a detriment. Thus, the purpose of this book is to provide some organized, structured guidance on the processes, pitfalls, and obstacles faced when serving as a thesis or dissertation Chair.

Much of the advice and insights are applicable to committee members as well. We have infused our own experiences as thesis and dissertation advisors throughout this book as a means to bring real people to the pages.

The chapters stand alone; that is, each chapter can be read out of order and out of context and still be meaningful in application. Each chapter begins with a basic case study and a set of reflective questions that spans the extent of the book and allows the reader to trace the path of a new committee Chair. In addition, each chapter features applicable real-life case in point scenarios to help illustrate the complexity of the relationship and processes of the thesis and dissertation. Last, each chapter features a set of "Points to Consider" or bulleted items that summarize the core content in each chapter and provide some thoughtful questions for the reader to consider after reading the content and considering how to apply it in real life.

Chapter One

Ten Questions to Ask Before Accepting Your First Chair Assignment

Authors' Note: We begin each chapter from this point on with a case study that spans the next ten chapters. The case study traces the path of a new Chair as she navigates her own expectations as well as those of the student and institution. The case study then leads to a series of questions to think about before reading each chapter. Envision yourself in the Chair's shoes and reflect on how you would best address each question both prior to and after reading the chapter.

CASE STUDY—PART 1

The new assistant professor was settling textbooks on the old office shelves. Catching sight of a self-reflection in the window glass, it was amazing to think that someone who was studying these books a year ago had been hired to teach this to others. The curriculum and classes were a familiar path to follow, but the role of Chair for graduate students' dissertations and theses was uncomfortable and unknown. None of the books on the shelves were very helpful on that point, and most of the advice from the other faculty was folk humor or anecdotes. How did one gain the knowledge and confidence to guide the students soon to come knocking on the door?

- *What formal and informal tools are available to learn the skills of Chair?*
- *What decisions are the Chair's to make, and what is decided by others in the process?*

Leading a student's thesis or dissertation committee is a serious yet reward-ing commitment. Some institutions allow students to create and invite com-mittee members of their choice while other institutions assign faculty to specific committee positions. Regardless of whether you are chairing a com-mittee by choice or by obligation, it is best to contemplate several things before beginning the process.

This list of "Ten Questions to Ask Before Accepting Your First Chair Assignment" provides thoughtful, engaging prompts to consider as you enter this new adventure:

1. WHO IS THE STUDENT?

Some Chairs enter the thesis or dissertation process with a familiar student, someone who has taken a class or has become known through personal or professional connections. Some Chairs enter into committee assignments with complete strangers. As a first step, it is important to do a bit of back-ground research on the student. That is, what appear to be the student's academic strengths and weaknesses? What topic area is the student explor-ing? What experiences have other faculty members reported having with the student?

It is not necessary to become overly investigative into a student's life, but it helps to have some background knowledge on the student's professional career, academic life, and scholarly promise before agreeing to any commit-tee work. Take time to ask questions of both the students and faculty at the institution. Seek to understand how the student will work through this highly independent and challenging process. Explore the student's professional goals with what you can offer as a mentor. By building a strong understand-ing of the student before ever committing to serve as a Chair, you are serving not only yourself, but the student well.

2. WHAT ARE THE INSTITUTION'S EXPECTATIONS OF A CHAIR?

There seems to be no one clear answer to exactly what colleges and univer-sities require of today's thesis and dissertation Chairs. Some institutions create manuals or other guiding documents, while others rely on tradition and word of mouth to relay important information. Before accepting a committee assignment, ask about the specific requirements for being a Chair at your institution. Are Chairs expected to serve as line editors of the paper? Do Chairs convene all meetings and submit all paperwork? Are there roles de-fined for committee members? There may be no written guidance, but it is imperative that if there is, you know what it is and can adhere to it throughout the process.

3. WHERE CAN I FIND POLICIES AND PROCEDURES REGARDING THE PROCESS?

Most colleges and universities maintain a set of policies and procedures regarding the academic progress of the thesis or dissertation student. That is, there will often be time lines and deadlines that must be met in order for a student to propose or defend a final paper. There will be required signatures for a variety of forms needed to attest to progress and to apply for graduation. Most of these policies can be found in the catalog of the institution, sometimes found in paper form, but usually found online in today's campus setting.

It is important to note that most campuses adhere to a policy utilizing the catalog from the date of the student's entrance into the program—that is, a student who began her master's degree in 2016 is held to the policies and procedures in place at the time when she entered the program. Changes made after that date may or may not apply, and it is important to ask to be sure to adhere to any updated protocols or processes.

4. WHO CAN I TURN TO FOR HELP?

The thesis and dissertation can be a lonely one for the student, but it can also be equally isolating for the Chair. Before agreeing to Chair a committee, find out who is available to help on the various known and unknown issues that arise during the process. This includes:

- Who manages the paperwork within the administrative offices?
- Who can direct you to the appropriate policies and procedures?
- What campus resources are available to assist the student with writing, counseling, or advising issues?
- Who can help you understand the layout of the thesis or dissertation required at this institution?
- Who can provide assistance with methodology if needed?
- What library resources are available to the student? Do you have access to those as well?

5. IN WHAT FORM OR FORMAT DOES A THESIS OR DISSERTATION NEED TO BE AT THIS UNIVERSITY?

The format of the thesis or dissertation may vary depending on institution, department, or preferences of faculty members. Before agreeing to serve as a Chair, try to find examples of student work that have met the department's requirements. Are there tools or templates available for student use? Is there a standard format all papers must meet or is there latitude for the Chair to help the student devise a nontraditional format? Search ProQuest for student examples within the field he or she is seeking to study and ensure that the format of the proposed study will not meet difficulties at the proposal or defense stages.

6. HOW DO I KNOW WHAT I DON'T KNOW? (AND WHAT IF SOMEONE FINDS OUT WHAT I DON'T KNOW?)

Before accepting a Chair assignment, one must acknowledge the unknown. Each student brings unique challenges and opportunities; learning new processes and policies, this time from the faculty side, can be a learning curve, and learning to expect the unexpected can be a reasonable rule to live by as a Chair. This is why asking questions is so important.

Make connections with faculty in the institution. Find colleagues who are also serving as Chairs and seek their advice. Attend student defenses for committees on which you do not serve just to observe the role of the Chair. The role of Chair is more than sitting back and waiting for the student to submit work. As your student researches and writes, so too, should you. Learn about the student's topic. Study the same articles. Assure the student that you are an engaged scholar.

7. DOES THE METHODOLOGY AND TOPIC THE STUDENT HOPES TO USE FIT MY EXPERTISE?

The methodology of a study can make or break your role as Chair. Ask the student to identify the type of methodology he or she is considering using for the thesis or dissertation. If it is a methodology with which you are unfamiliar, how will you learn the skills in order to ensure that the study is sound? Are there resources available to help students with research design? Most of all, are you capable of learning a research design that you may not have worked with in the past?

This is an important step of self-realization; sometimes a committee assignment is accepted only to learn that the Chair is learning the research design alongside the student. Build on your strengths—if a student is proposing a study with a design you have never studied or utilized, consider your alternatives. You may put a method specialist on the committee as reader, with the understanding that this person will take the lead on questions about method until the design is accepted by the committee. You can decline or request to be reader, not Chair, on the committee. If you are expert in the topic, you can learn about unfamiliar designs. It is harder to have no expertise in the field of the topic. Again, a specialist could be assigned as reader, but it may be best to explore the avenue of cochairing with an experienced faculty member.

8. DO I HAVE TIME FOR THIS?

Personal workload and well-being should be analyzed before accepting a Chair assignment. That is, really look at your life. Examine your commitments. Do you have not only time to commit to this process, but *quality* time? Do you have availability to meet with the student? To review multiple drafts? To assist with writing challenges? To listen to the student's concerns and complaints? To schedule and plan the committee meetings? Can you still focus on your own well-being in the midst of this added commitment to your life? If so, find a way to add it to your overall balance.

9. DO I WANT TO DO THIS?

In addition to finding the time and having the academic ability to serve as a Chair, take time to meaningfully reflect on whether you really want to serve as a Chair. Do you want to invest in a student in this way? Do you have a passion for learning that will extend over the course of months or years? Can you mentor this student personally and professionally? Do you have a strong writing background to help the student grow as a writer?

Being able to research and write well is an entirely different set of skills from teaching someone else to research and write. A Chair who only writes for the student or hands them another dissertation, saying, "Do it like this," is too laissez-faire to benefit the student. Can you provide encouragement in times of stress? Chairing a thesis or dissertation is not for everyone. It may be that you are assigned to serve as a Chair as part of your workload; how can you find ways to connect with the process to find personal and professional fulfillment rather than viewing it as a path to promotion and tenure?

10. WHAT AM I BRINGING FROM MY OWN EXPERIENCES INTO THIS?

The one commonality we all bring into the Chair position is our own experiences as a thesis or dissertation student. Some of these were wonderful memories. Some were traumatic events. Think about your time as a student. How did you manage the workload, isolation, and demands of writing your paper? How did you interact with your Chair? What frustrations arose during the process? How did you navigate unexpected roadblocks? What we bring from our own experiences as a student can be extremely helpful to a student or can be a continuation of dysfunction. Reflect on how your journey will impact your new journey as a Chair.

Chapter Two

Being a Chair

CASE STUDY—PART 2

Taking on the first committee assignment, Chair was excited to begin this new academic adventure with Student. Chair had come to know Student informally through some coursework and departmental functions. Chair began to daydream about how the committee would work—the vibrant interactions, scholarly discussions, and thoughtful reading of drafts. Chair remembered her days as a graduate student and how her Chair had motivated and challenged. Chair also remembered the difficulties of the writing process, the isolation of hours and hours spent writing, and the almost nonexistent input from a committee member. This would be different. Chair knew this experience would go seamlessly and quickly dismissed the bumps and potholes of past experience.

- *How can a new Chair understand the responsibilities and demands of serving as a thesis or dissertation Chair?*
- *What considerations should Chair be thinking about before accepting a committee assignment, if in fact, she can choose to accept or deny serving?*
- *Who is Chair responsible to during the thesis or dissertation process?*
- *What should Chairs consider about their own leadership style before engaging in this type of committee work?*

Serving as a thesis or dissertation Chair is an extremely important task in academia across the nation and throughout the world. Leading a student scholar through this final phase of original research is often challenging, time consuming, and yet quite rewarding. Today, over 50,000 doctoral degrees are issued each year (National Science Foundation, 2018). This means that thesis and dissertation chairpersons are integral in the advancement of the academy and necessary to continue to build an ongoing base of scholars. In addition, within the past ten years, many online institutions have implemented hiring practices that utilize high numbers of adjunct or remote chairpersons to lead thesis or dissertation committees.

Many Chairs are unprepared to lead a thesis or dissertation committee without some guidance from the institution itself. In fact, quite frequently, the Chair's only experience with a thesis or dissertation was his or her own— meaning the Chair carries the habits, practices, and expectations of a completely different set of people and institutional norms. As most teachers are aware, the practice of teaching is much different from being a student in the class. So, too, is leading the thesis or dissertation process. As institutions, we expect faculty to readily embrace and lead theses or dissertations effectively with little or no guidance beyond some minor procedural deadlines and guidelines.

This book is to help support and guide Chairs on the ins and outs of leading a thesis or dissertation committee. We, as thesis and dissertation Chairs ourselves, recognize the need for specific guidance and best practices that are readily implementable and apply to a broad range of institutions. We, too, have shared experiences from both our own dissertations and guiding graduate students through the processes.

Not every student we have advised has succeeded, which led us to realize that if the Chair is not part of a department conversation on thesis or dissertation processes, or relies exclusively on personal experience as a graduate student, the student may miss important information about the processes involved in this important final step in a graduate career. While the content of this book may be general in nature, it does apply to a variety of disciplines and can be widely understood and applied by Chairs in a variety of content areas. While specific disciplines may have unique customs or demands, the process itself can be led in a universal way that builds support for students, protects academic integrity, and hopefully leads to a successful outcome.

So, why study these best practices to leading dissertation and thesis committees? Why not replicate your own experience (good or bad)? Why not just wing it and hope the student gets through? Overall, there are four key players that rely on the academic integrity and scholarly nature of the thesis and dissertation process: the student, the institution, the field of study, and you.

THE IMPORTANCE TO THE STUDENT

The student is the primary focus in the thesis or dissertation process. After all, it is the student who assumes a majority of the responsibility, from generating a topic to designing original research to defending a publishable final manuscript. As independent as a graduate student may be, he or she relies on the advice and guidance of the Chair to successfully defend a thesis or dissertation.

Often, the thesis or dissertation process is the first time in a graduate program that the student may be independent and out of a traditional course structure. In addition, the student is being asked to produce work in a format that may be completely new—sometimes designing a new research study for a thesis or dissertation is a student's initial attempt at doing so. Last, students often face a new type of ambiguity, one in which the answers to problems cannot be found in textbooks or located quickly in a database. Ambiguity can often induce stress, sometimes in an amount previously not experienced by relatively successful graduate students.

The Chair, then, is integral as a guide for the student through the thesis or dissertation process. The Chair not only teaches, advises, listens, and coaches, but also shepherds the process, carefully leading the student through the necessary steps to select a topic, design a research method, and conduct meaningful research. Sometimes the Chair is the only connection a student has to the university and may be the only person able to answer questions about the process or product. Additionally, the Chair often holds a fair share of content knowledge necessary to ensure that the student adheres to the applicable scholarship in the field being studied. The student will reach out to the Chair with questions, concerns, or difficulties.

Sometimes the Chair is seen more as a coach, encouraging students to muddle through the difficulty of data collection and writing drafts, while other times the Chair is an authoritarian figure offering strict deadlines to ensure a study is completed in a timely fashion. This wavering, from supporter to enforcer, can be confusing for a Chair and can often be an emotional rollercoaster. We hope the guidance provided in this book will help provide some structure to your role and offer some support as to how to handle some contentious student or committee relationships.

> *Case in point: Tom recently successfully passed his thesis proposal and is ready to move on to his defense. He was allowed to select his chair, Dr. P, from within a department of 10 qualified professors. Tom had taken a couple classes with Dr. P and felt her expertise would align well with his study.*
>
> *When Tom set up an initial meeting with Dr. P to discuss his thesis ideas, she shared that this was the first thesis for which she had served as a Chair and that she was unsure about the deadlines or paperwork Tom would need to complete to earn his master's degree. Tom left the meeting unsure that he*

made the right choice. While Dr. P was a strong academic and knew a lot about his topic, he was not sure she knew enough about the process to get him to graduation in a timely manner. He left worried, confused, and unsure as to what his next step should be.

As a Chair, leadership is crucial. The student depends on you for guidance. The institution relies on you to ensure that academic prowess is alive, and your professional reputation can be tied to a student's work. Be prepared to lead—that is, be prepared to have an opinion, speak up when something is not going as planned, and to disagree. This leadership may be difficult and may, at times, be political, but it is necessary to be an effective advocate for the graduate student.

THE IMPORTANCE TO THE INSTITUTION

Colleges and universities rely on graduate students to build a new generation of scholars and future academics. Not only are graduate programs usually profitable, often due to the receipt of fellowships or grants, but the reputation of an institution is tied to a student's final product. The institution, be it a college or university, seeks quality academic research and relies on the Chair to be the gatekeeper for the quality of institutional products. Universities may use the thesis or dissertation process to uncover new research, innovative ideas, or new, exciting findings, while others may use the process to generate a highly educated alumni population.

The expansion of graduate programs into the online sphere has added new opportunities for access to education previously unseen when students had to attend face-to-face class or write a dissertation while serving in a residency on campus. Some programs still require more formal contact during the thesis or dissertation process, but some online universities hire Chairs from external sources as adjuncts and train them to lead the thesis or dissertation process remotely. As such, Chairs are no longer situated in ivory towers on campus. Some may not actively teach at a university. Some may be professionals in practice, adding a unique facet to exactly who is qualified to lead a thesis or dissertation committee.

Because the institution relies heavily on the professionalism of a Chair, it only makes sense that the institution should provide some direction on professional standards, guidelines, and ethical expectations for the thesis and dissertation process as well. However, few universities do this, generally finding qualified (by a certain earned degree and professional experience) as the only prerequisite to leading a dissertation committee. When a university is so reliant on one person, the Chair, it is also liable when misconduct occurs or ethical guidelines are avoided. From an institutional standpoint, the more training and guidance a Chair receives, the more assurance there is that the final product is one worthy of the institution's seal of approval.

THE IMPORTANCE TO THE FIELD OF STUDY

A thesis or dissertation is generally considered an original contribution to an existing field of study. Students are challenged to "find the gap" in academic literature in order to design a narrow topic that can be studied through an original research design. Even for student research that replicates the research of others, new information emerges and a field of study is advanced.

The integrity of student research, particularly that in the thesis or dissertation process, is integral to the advancement of the academic field studied. That is, new scholars often offer new insights and different ways to look at problems, and are preparing themselves to conduct future studies. Accordingly, the Chair is also responsible to the field—that is, by chairing a thesis or dissertation, you are the chief oversight that the student's research process is sound and the findings are applicable and real. Failure to see this importance is a limited scope of responsibility. While it may seem highly unlikely that the entire field of physics or education relies on you, you are an integral piece in the construction of the field of study.

> ***Case in point:*** *Dr. S's department of music education had been gathering data for several years on professional dispositions of preservice music educators. Tabitha's experience as a music educator in several different settings over the past decade gave her a new lens to study this topic. She replicated a well-established department study to explore dispositions of veteran music educators, and the findings led not only to a deeper, broader view of professional dispositions but also to improvements in the master's program at the university.*

THE IMPORTANCE TO THE CHAIR

Chairing a thesis or dissertation may be a task to complete a service requirement within your promotion and tenure dossier or it may be a requirement of your faculty role within a department. Regardless of what causes you to serve as a thesis or dissertation Chair, this relationship you form with the student, the process you lead, and the outcome of the student's work is (or should be) important to you as a professional. After all, you are signing your name to the work and when the work is published, readers will see that you were the Chair of the committee that signed off on the work. Work that is inaccurate, unethical, or poorly constructed can be tied to you professionally and may tarnish the reputation you have worked hard to build. Work that is stellar can reflect a strong scholar, engaging teacher, and contributor to the field.

The Chair role is one that allows you to exercise leadership and help a student emerge into a scholar. This can be very rewarding, yet also very challenging. The thesis and dissertation process can be time consuming, may not add anything to your professional profile, and may simply be something you do because you are interested in the topic being studied. However, the level of responsibility, from assisting a student wandering through the unknown to protecting an institution's reputation, rests on your shoulders. It is not a decision that should be entered lightly, but one that should be considered carefully at the inception of each committee. Think through how you want students to remember you as their Chair—as encouraging? Demanding? Authoritarian? Unresponsive? It is really up to you to determine which direction you want to go and how your role as a Chair will evolve.

THE CHAIR AS LEADER

Accepting the responsibility of chairing a thesis or dissertation should be a decision made with deliberation and reflection on one's own leadership abilities. One piece that seems to be overlooked a bit is the acknowledgment of leadership skills necessary to lead a committee—often from scholars and faculty who have little formal leadership training. Depending on your leadership style, you may or may not find the Chair experience to be a fruitful or enjoyable one. Before entering this process, determine how you lead best. Amanchukwu, Stanley, and Ololube (2015) outline some basic leadership styles, which we have used to conceptualize how the styles might apply to a thesis or dissertation committee setting:

a. *Autocratic* Leadership Style: Sometimes considered "authoritarian," this type of leader demands to be in charge and to make decisions. As a Chair, this type of leadership trait can be efficient in that the direction of the committee is clear and little input from others is needed. However, this type of leadership also tends to remove ownership from the student and fosters a dependence on the Chair that may preclude the scholar from making independent decisions about the study he or she is proposing.

b. *Bureaucratic* Leadership Style: These leaders follow the rules and heavily rely on the rules for direction. In an institutional setting, this can ensure that all of the requirements to progress toward graduation are met. However, this type of leadership can also stifle creativity and limit flexibility.

c. *Charismatic* Leadership Style: Sometimes referred to as "transformational leadership," this type of leader inspires the best in others. The leader is easy to follow and enthusiastic; followers are excited to work on the project. As a Chair, this type of leadership can be inspirational to the student and can help breathe life into otherwise dull moments. However, this type of leadership also requires a heavy reliance on the leader to remain consistently enthused, which can be a difficult trait to keep long term in the midst of busy lives.

d. *Democratic/Participative* Leadership Style: This leadership style involves others in the decision making. As a Chair, it could mean allowing each committee member to have a say in the process and study formation as well as utilizing student input before any final decision is made. This style probably fits thesis or dissertation committees well but can also be difficult to manage; if everyone has an opinion, the process can drag on and meaningful decisions can be delayed until consensus can be reached.

e. *Laissez-Faire* Leadership Style: Laissez-faire leadership can be a blessing or a nightmare to a student. This is an "anything goes" mentality and requires very little decision making on the part of the leader. It also requires a high level of independence by the student. As a Chair, it may be difficult to maintain this leadership style and still meet deadlines and ensure that institutional requirements are met. This type of leadership is also what tends to irritate students the most—that is, most students need some sort of guidance and if left on their own to make all decisions, probably do so in a uninformed manner.

f. *Transactional* Leadership Style: This leadership style relies on some sort of "transaction" to occur in the leader/follower relationship. Within a committee setting, this might be the sense of obligation a Chair feels to get a student to graduation or to serve on a committee in order to earn promotion and tenure. This leader probably also uses rewards and punishment as a means of motivation. In a committee setting, some of these rewards or punishments might be subtle, such as the delay in reading a draft because a student failed to meet a deadline or eagerly promoting the student's work to others when a request by the leader has been incorporated into the student's work. Some students will be motivated by this type of leadership, while others will be unfazed.

Again, there is no one right or wrong way to lead a committee. In fact, different stages of the thesis or dissertation may require employing different leadership styles. However, it is important to determine what your leadership style is and to share that with the committee and the student. This type of honest discussion can help alleviate concerns about how the committee will operate and will allow committee members to share their own leadership preferences—which in turn will signal the various leadership styles present in the committee structure.

POINTS TO CONSIDER

- Remember that it is more than the student who relies on the Chair during the thesis or dissertation process. The committee, institution, field of study, and the Chair's professional reputation can be affected.
- Understand that universities rely on Chairs to serve as gatekeepers of quality and integrity.
- Acknowledge that prior experience as a master's or doctoral student is not sufficient to ensure expertise as a Chair. Be open to learning about the process and best practices in order to help ensure student success.
- There may or may not be a choice to serve as a committee Chair. Regardless of choice in the matter, consider the ethical and academic strengths and how to be immersed in the committee process.
- Understand that Chairs serve in different capacities depending on the institution. Be prepared to ask questions about processes and norms in order to understand what will be expected of the student with whom you are working.
- The stress and workload of serving as a Chair is often unacknowledged. Conflict will arise, time management will be crucial, and you may be faced with questions that you cannot answer. Accept this—a Chair is not expected to be an expert on everything. Share the inquiry process alongside the student. Look for positive experiences and teachable moments in each committee.

Chapter Three

Crafting of the Committee

CASE STUDY—PART 3

Chair began thinking about who the ideal committee members for Student's committee might be. Dr. Pompous would be a noteworthy member because of his reputation in the field, but he was also known for lacking time to provide student feedback. Dr. Disorder was an enthusiastic faculty member, but the piles and piles of papers stacked in her office made Chair wonder if Student would find a place in one of those piles. Dr. Grammar was a solid writer and would ensure that the student's final paper was error free, but also focused a lot more on spelling than on theory and methodology. Department Chair suggested that Dr. Unknown might be a good fit for the committee based on his work experience, but Chair had never met Dr. Unknown. Student suggested Dr. Friendly, who was passionate about the content area, but also known for her easy grading and student-friendly class conversations.

- *How should Chair determine the best fit for the student's committee?*
- *What unknown aspects of committee formation might Chair be overlooking?*
- *How can Chair bring such different personalities to the table to accomplish the common goal of shepherding the student to graduation?*

Chairing a committee means undertaking many responsibilities for the graduate student, but this task is complicated because it requires committee approval to be successful. The more people involved, the more skills become necessary for implementing a vision, negotiating wants from needs, and respectfully resolving conflicts. A Chair must understand the norms and policies surrounding the work of the committee, the roles that committee members take, and the leadership of a diverse group with strong opinions.

A COMMITTEE AS AN ORGANIZATION

A thesis or dissertation committee is a group of experts who support the writing and completion of a new work of research. While any group has unique purposes and personalities, the nature of a dissertation or thesis committee makes examination of committee formation interesting. The committee is a formal group with an assigned leader, yet it is also a relatively short-term group, with few meetings and one objective. The central group member, the graduate student, comes from outside this faculty group and often has little or no experience of the patterns and expectations of the group, and just as critically, is unaware of the interplay or the long-term interactions between the other group members.

There are basic stages of group development that can guide the crafting of a successful dissertation or thesis committee. These broad, general stages have been well defined by Tuckman (1965). All groups do not go through these stages linearly, but the basic pattern is:

- forming (testing-dependence),
- storming (conflict),
- norming (cohesion), and
- performing (function; Tuckman, 1965).

Whether the Chair recruits or inherits the committee members, being in charge of the committee is sometimes as much an art as it is a science.

FORMING A COMMITTEE

Creation of a committee is bound by the traditions of the college and the policies of the graduate school. This process can be as informal as requiring the candidate to contact graduate faculty to request their participation, or as formal as assignment of committee positions by the university administration, then informing the candidate of the team. Those who follow a student-choice process have the benefits of initial candidate satisfaction with the members and less bureaucracy in the formation, but soon may be faced with committees that do not include the best support for the candidate, field, or research—and one whose members may not work well with one another. On the other hand, when the institution initiates the selection of committees, candidates may not have an initial trusting relationship, or department selection criteria may prioritize equal workload over candidate needs.

Each college's traditions and policies usually set this process somewhere on the continuum between these extremes. For example, a student-choice process may include a step of submitting a list of potential committee members for approval by department chair, and a university-chosen process could be assignment of the Chair for the thesis or dissertation, then the Chair and candidate together invite the other members. Committee formation policy and tradition varies across majors, over time, and with changes in faculty.

To make it even more complex, the role of the Chair in the committee also has its own traditions at each site. These range from the autonomous Chair with other committee members playing subordinate roles, to the other extreme where the role of the Chair is to coordinate the committee members who collaborate on various tasks, and all advise the candidate. When the Chair's role and the selection process are considered simultaneously, four broad dimensions of committees emerge:

- Mentor—student selected, autonomous role
- Master—institution selected, autonomous role
- Mosaic—student selected, team role
- Machine—institution selected, team role

Knowing which of these dimensions is in play before starting to chair helps to step outside the immediate issues presented by the student and study to preempt pitfalls.

Mentor

When students select an autonomous Chair, candidates gravitate toward someone to guide them whom they know and like. They seek expertise and advising from a role model who knows the field and type of research.

> ***Case in point:*** *During her classes, Marie listened to others in her program on the merits of her choices for dissertation Chair. She did not think too much about the other members of her committee, except to choose people who were easy to get along with and positive toward her. But the Chair was the big decision. Some of her peers shared their stories about the expectations of their Chairs, so Marie knew she wanted a friendly person who cared about the students.*
>
> *When she took Dr. C's class, she knew this was someone who would be patient with her and who had an interest in her topic. Dr. C was happy to chair Marie's committee, and they both enjoyed their discussions as Marie narrowed her topic and began to organize her literature.*
>
> *As time went along, Marie was sometimes frustrated with the slow feedback from Dr. C. She knew that Dr. C was very busy because many candidates were working with her, but when the feedback finally arrived, the suggestions were worthwhile and helpful. The farther she got in the process, the more*

*Marie noticed that her work reflected Dr. C's opinions, and she worried what
the rest of the committee would think of the proposal. Should she reach out to
them, or would Dr. C see that as disloyal?*

As with Marie, mentoring focuses the dissertation development in the
interplay of the Chair and candidate. Open communication and transparent
objectives, time lines, and goals help to avoid many conflicts, and a Chair
who has an awareness of mentoring beyond giving advice and evaluations
fosters the relationship as well as the research. Cognitive coaching (Costa &
Garmston, 2016) provides a mindset and strategies in mentoring that result in
pushing candidate thinking. Coaching strategies include meditative questioning, facilitating thinking without placing judgment, probing for clarity, paraphrasing, and using wait time for reflection. Intentional application of these
strategies in discussions with candidates not only allows the candidate concrete direction in his or her own thinking, but it also gives the mentoring
Chair specific tactics to use in channeling work in a positive direction.

A mentoring relationship becomes problematic when the boundaries between professionalism and friendship are not clearly set. A student who
phones a Chair on Sunday afternoon to announce arrival at the Chair's home
in the next hour (and does not see why the Chair declines the meeting) is
depending on the friendship that develops and allowing it to lead to un-
healthy forms of dependence. Setting ground rules is important so that there
is less chance for misunderstanding on either side.

As the mentor and candidate have worked through the research process
together, it can become difficult to keep the rest of the committee involved in
decisions. When committee members are advisory rather than active, role
ambiguity should be addressed. Too often, other committee members bring
up points at proposal or defense that would have been useful much earlier in
the decision making. Having checkpoints with the committee in the planning
stages allows their expertise to be utilized rather than having a committee
merely for evaluation of complete work.

Master

Sometimes the institution assigns the Chair. In this case, the topic is usually
predetermined as part of a larger body of the institution's research and the
Chair is deemed the most knowledgeable in the field. These Chairs are also
role models for the work, and often the dissertation or thesis is tangential or
complementary to their own research. The candidate has the benefit of knowing that the work will have academic merit and broader significance and has
the security of apprenticing to an expert.

Unfortunately, some experts are not also expert teachers and expect the
novice to catch on merely by observation or emulation, and in other cases

have expectations that the finished work reverts to the Chair's body of work rather than launching the candidate's own scholarship path. Students need a clear pathway to discuss problems with the department and know the policy for changing Chairs in situations where they are not able to meet the expectations or even the idiosyncrasies of an assigned Chair. Sometimes another committee member may also assume a master's role with the graduate student. When this happens, the Chair needs to discuss concerns with the member directly, and not expect the student to try to serve two masters or negotiate between two opinions.

Mosaic

When the candidate solicits the involvement of all committee members, the Chair receives a group known to the candidate and often chosen from acquaintance rather than expertise. This allows the student to have several sympathetic advisors or editors. It also can create a "blind men and the elephant" of a paper when each member brings a separate set of skills and preferences without a cohesive whole. When multiple people have active roles in a dissertation or thesis, communication is improved if the Chair receives a copy of all feedback to coordinate and negotiate with and for the student.

Sometimes student-chosen committees have too-similar areas of expertise. If, for example, all members are strong in their field but not experienced in chairing novice research, the project may become overambitious. If all members are from a close group, groupthink can weaken the results. The Chair can assign roles to the committee members for better working conditions, and even add another committee member if the group would improve with more expertise.

Machine

Some graduate students, especially graduate assistants, are part of a faculty work team. The new study is part of the greater work being accomplished by the team, and the committee members are also fellow researchers. Support for this thesis or dissertation is easily at hand for the student and being the junior member of the team brings unique challenges for the student.

> ***Case in point:*** *Mark was initially thrilled to work with Dr. Q's group on an exciting thesis topic. He worked hard and completed his study in record time. At his oral defense, Mark proudly presented his findings and was expecting accolades. Instead a noisy argument erupted among the committee members. Mark was largely ignored while the others carried on what seemed to be a long-standing argument.*

> *When Mark's committee did not pass him, he was bewildered as to how to move forward. If he satisfied one committee member, he would offend another. If he did not make the changes, he would not graduate. Mark believed in his work and the conclusions he was proposing, and he could not afford to start over with another topic, but he felt he was in the crosshairs of a faculty dispute.*

When a team approach is used, students like Mark get not only the glory of the group, but also the baggage. Meeting with the full committee before starting the process allows the Chair to predict and prevent problems while creating boundaries between the thesis/dissertation and the overall research of the team.

Storming Toward Consensus

Once a committee is formed, the group works to understand the scope and the limitations of the work. When a dissertation or thesis committee is formed of people with different graduate school experiences and philosophies, assumptions that the new group will act in accordance with previous experiences cause conflict. Each committee, and each study, has its own problems to solve, but there are common understandings and conflict resolutions that a Chair usually navigates.

Roles for a Successful Committee

A graduate student gets to the research phase of the degree with a variety of experiences in writing, conducting research, reasoning, and synthesizing knowledge for interpretation. While the building of these skills is foundational to dissertation and thesis writing, constructing the project from beginning to end also presents the student with new challenges. It is said that if all you have is a hammer, everything looks like a nail. Those without a broad research background may not even be aware of the breadth of literature, variety of framework, choices of methods, or availability of tools. A committee needs to combine the elements to guide the student through these new challenges to insights and to support refining of skills.

A Chair needs to be realistic and understand that one cannot be all things to all people. When building the committee, support needs to be in place for the background and the theoretical or conceptual framework. A methodologist should be handy to be sure that the proposed work has a refined question and alignment with instruments. Oversight of writing for flow and organization is just as important as providing editing and revising. As members complement one another, sharing the progress as well as the burden makes the work lighter for the candidate.

Candidates Test Limits

During the storming phase, it is human nature to test the rules and the authority. When a candidate says, "But it's *my* study!" the conflict is engaged. If early in the classes graduate students learn that the dissertation or thesis has processes and procedures in place for the protection of the novice researcher, a second explanation should be made that those who successfully navigate the project do so by cooperating with the committee. Those learning to ride a bike may feel limited by training wheels, but they are also protected by them. The dissertation and thesis have similar restrictions and regulations to protect the university, Chair, and graduate student.

Trying to play one committee member against another is not an uncommon reaction to critical feedback. If the Chair is transparent about the reasons for the requirements and shares information between members so the information is not reinterpreted by the candidate, power struggles can be minimized.

Committee Members Question Process

Much of the storming comes from committee members trying to be helpful. Some types of help are appreciated and positive, but help can also be camouflage for intrusion and interference. Conflicts of interest arise from differences in needs, goals, or values; scarcity of resources including power, popularity, and position; and issues of rivalry (Johnson & Johnson, 2016). Embracing the idea that conflict is normal can keep a Chair from the endless task of attempting to eliminate it and point toward more positive efforts.

Having no conflict in a group turns it toward complacency and apathy, but too much conflict descends into chaos. A Chair who avoids or suppresses all conflict as well as one who ignores or promotes disharmony is only aggravating the problem and the group.

Conflict management becomes the responsibility of the Chair as group leader. Asking a member to play devil's advocate can inject constructive conflict to avoid groupthink. Reducing destructive conflict can be more problematic. According to the Thomas-Kilmann Conflict Mode Instrument (2002), the response to conflict can be determined by the assertiveness and cooperativeness involved. Responses are:

- Avoiding—this should be done when the problem is petty or one that others should solve.
- Accommodating—when power is low, others must be accommodated, and if the other cares about a nonessential matter, accommodating is efficient.
- Compromising—this maintains harmony, but is minimally acceptable to all.

- Collaborating—this occurs when there is time and reason for the work of achieving a win/win solution.
- Forcing—win/lose is necessary when enforcing policies for the safety of others.

Analysis of conflict from a theory-based plan rather than an emotional reaction increases the odds of a successful and satisfying outcome. If destructive conflict is continuing, following the strategies in guides such as *Fierce Conversations* (Scott, 2017) or *Crucial Conversations* (Patterson, Grenny, McMillan, & Switzler, 2012) can be of immense help to a Chair.

NORMING THE GROUP

Not all committees experience the storming stage of group development, but all engage in norming as they work toward consensus and tolerate the variance among the members. A dissertation/thesis committee understands that its purpose is to guide the student to a successful defense, and that the failure of the student is also a failure for the committee. The university and departments support this consensus building through guidelines, policies, handbooks, and procedures for the structure and quality of the product. Around all of the stated rules are the norms formed through tradition that create a pattern of expected behaviors for both student and faculty.

Interpreting Policies and Procedures

New Chairs must familiarize themselves with all the regulatory aspects a candidate is likely to encounter. These provide a safety net not just for the student, but for the Chair. Being able to quote the graduate catalog ends attempts to stretch rules and allows the Chair to point to a higher authority to guide the student. Policies the Chair should know are found in the graduate catalog, IRB application, department handbooks, university materials and website, and the thesis/dissertation publisher's guide. When policies contradict one another, the highest authority prevails. Just as the U.S. Supreme Court interprets the Constitution, the Chair interprets the meaning of the policies for the student. A wise Chair follows policy strictly to avoid setting a poor precedent for future committees.

Collaborating to Improve the Unwritten Rules

Who speaks first in a meeting, whether questions are asked during or after the defense presentation, how long students can expect to wait for a reply email from the Chair, and thousands of other unwritten rules, or norms, define how Chairs and students navigate the process from idea to publication.

Edgar Schein (2017) defines cultural norms as the way we do things around here, and because norms are only observed, not policy that is written or discussed, they are open for misinterpretation.

As students follow what they see in their classmates, they may miss the purpose and go through the motions into dead-end behaviors. It is noticeable when a candidate primarily uses other theses or dissertations as a model that the weaknesses of the initial paper or format become amplified in the new paper. Norms are also observable in where committee members sit at the table, what kinds of questions are accepted as topics, or how the research site and author are referred to in the paper. While ranging from petty to crucial, when there is disagreement on what is the proper way, the Chair needs to clarify the difference between a personal preference and an unwritten rule, and if norms are under discussion they need to be defined and explained.

Keeping Norms Current

The norms of completing a thesis or dissertation were developed in a time when students lived on campus, worked full-time on their degree, and moved from one level of graduate work to another with little intervening time. The current reality of graduate students is very different from the traditional, and so new norms and policies have to be in place.

Distance Students

Living in a digital age means that students have access to a wide variety of online tools for writing, gathering, and analyzing data, and for advice for the dissertation or thesis. Electronic library services offer not only a massive amount of available literature, but also guides, tutorials, and systems to support graduate students.

Electronic learning also offers students the opportunity to study at distant campuses that they can seldom or never attend face-to-face. Chairing a dissertation online adds greater emphasis on intentional relationship building. Just as it is easier to be curt or discourteous to a phone salesperson than one at the door, it is easier for the Chair, committee members, or student to interpret electronic messages more harshly than intended.

Even with video chatting, some elements of natural relationship building are difficult to achieve, and the distance is felt not in miles but in understanding one another. In these situations, it is imperative to check for meaning and intent of communications. Assuming that silence means displeasure or inactivity also brings conflict to the process. A Chair should have a routine of checking in with online and distance students, an articulated process for sending feedback in an expected manner, and the time to build the relationship beyond the dissertation or thesis tasks. Providing feedback can also be augmented by color coding messages.

If required edits and revisions are coded green, suggestions for changes in wording or organization blue, and asides or thought questions that do not need to be seen as a change in the paper as red, students do not spend time on trying to rewrite for casual comments and know that suggestions should be addressed in some way, but not necessarily as suggested. Candidates who are not distance students appreciate this coded feedback when revising as well.

International Students

When candidates are completing the research and writing in a second language, nuances and connotations can make comprehension of the literature and of the written work difficult. If the Chair is not also bilingual, committee support for writing in the content area is necessary. Sending students to a writing center or tutor can set sentences in standard English, but generic writing help is often not enough.

International students have also had an education that is different from the students native to the university nation. This provides great diversity for a program, and new perspectives to explore, but can cause the graduate student not to have the same prerequisite learning and skills that are taken for granted by faculty.

> *Case in point: Reemahna was a straight A student in her country as a child and undergraduate. She studied extremely hard to earn good grades in all her graduate classes. When she was asked to write formal papers or reflections, the professor would work to help her understand the idea of supporting a thesis not only with quotes, but with her own analysis. As she started the dissertation, this different perspective of writing made it impossible for her to show her expertise.*
>
> *In her earlier education, she was taught to cite experts whom she was to respect—and not to express her own understanding and interpretation. Her literature review looked like a string of block quotes and summaries without building an argument or logically organizing evidence and conclusions. Finally, Dr. K read her work aloud to her, stopping at appropriate points to ask Reemahna what she thought about the content, or why she chose to include the passage. As Dr. K wrote what she said, these formed the introductions and conclusions that she knew but did not feel she should put in the paper.*
>
> *It was the constant support of a graduate assistant in the same manner that allowed Reemahna to share what she was thinking in her writing. Her culture norm against evaluating or questioning authority would have made the work unacceptable in this culture. In the end, the work was hers, but learning to stand up for her opinions is still a work in progress.*

International students also need the Chair to have a relationship with the university's international programs and studies departments. They need support for visas and in adjusting time lines to meet the needs of their own nation's norms and calendars. Committee members should be selected who embrace diversity and are tolerant of differing worldviews. In some cultures, creating certificates with seals and letterheads with extra flourishes and signatures for the student to display is highly prized. By developing a close relationship with international students, a Chair has the opportunity to gain a more global perspective as well.

Part-Time Degrees

Television commercials recruit people to their programs by showing the busy parent on the computer at night holding a sleeping child or a tired worker commuting home and doing online assignments on the bus. It is attractive to think that graduate work can be slipped into the corners between a profession and family life and often the juggling is done successfully through the coursework phase of a program. When faced with completing a complex research and writing project, without the weekly deadlines and regular patterns of a class time line, too many students end up never finishing. Even though the Chair cannot shepherd the student to write, providing support in the form of books, articles, and websites about avoiding procrastination can help students find helpful strategies.

Generational Differences Complicating the Issues

There are many expressions of this, such as students who daily retweet messages may have different perspectives of what constitutes professional language or plagiarism than their committee. What seems to be cutting corners to a Chair may be merely being efficient to the student.

It is normal for those who have completed their degrees to be skeptical of those earning one, and for students to see all professors as dinosaurs. One generation does not need to become like the other to value the contributions of the other. For example, Chairs who judiciously add the appropriate emoji to their online feedback to students may find their messages are less sterile and have a warmer tone that improves the relationship. However, overuse may be cloying and condescending. Continuing to experiment with new strategies and supporting nontraditional, meritorious ideas stifles the tendency to do things the way they were done in the good old days.

On the other hand, there are professional standards of practice, research, language, and behavior that should be upheld. Earning a graduate degree implies an advanced and polished person will graduate to be respected by the peers in the field. Relaxing the requirements for professionalism may make a Chair popular for some, but not for most who are spending their time and effort to achieve an advanced degree. When all else fails, referring to the expectations of the committee can motivate a student to polish work in fear of rejection.

PERFORMING THE DEFENSE

The performing stage of a committee is steeped in tradition and lore. Students hear stories of the terrible experiences others have had in the past, true or not, and fear being humiliated or denied graduation. Setting the committee for student success includes not only selecting supportive faculty but also digging into any common problems that students have at this stage and creating a more positive culture in the future by addressing the problems. If a university has passed a person on all classes, and the Chair has recommended the candidate for defense, it is also his or her personal or systemic fault if he or she does not foresee major flaws, at least at the time the final draft is read so that rewriting can occur. Negative results from secretive committee deliberations are not a productive way to advertise the program to prospective students.

Preparing the Candidate for Proposal and Defense

The fact that candidates are eloquent writers does not mean that they are equally articulate presenters. A defense is not only a celebration of work completed, it is the beginning of sharing the findings.

> *Case in point: Oscar had sent his final draft to his committee, had his Power-Point slides for his oral defense approved by Dr. R, and had practiced his presentation and answers to possible questions. In his best suit, he started his presentation by clicking to his first slide. Suddenly, a loud car crash sound effect interrupted him. Rattled, he continued until flipping to the next slide which opened to a cow's moo.*
>
> *Oscar had to admit to his audience that he had borrowed his son's computer and asked him to add the visuals to the slides. Obviously, he got more than he bargained for, but he did not know how to mute the unfamiliar computer. Until technical support arrived, he had to present with a cacophony of sounds that reminded his snickering committee of animated cartoons.*

As Chair, it is not possible to foresee all missteps in preparing to present the final product. Candidate nerves, technical glitches, and rude audience members can all divert focus from the defense. There are, however, several points that a Chair should discuss and check before unleashing the committee on the candidate. Preparing the defense can include holding a practice session with other graduate students, sharing probable questions from committee members, and video recording practices for the candidate to see.

No one can answer all questions, nor should they think they need to know all the answers. Candidates can get themselves in trouble by being afraid to confess they do not know, so they say something that is disastrous instead. A few stock responses all candidates should have ready are:

- That's an interesting idea. It would be great for further study, so I'll add to that section.
- That was beyond the scope of my study, but it would be useful as another study.
- That was something the Chair and I discussed. We decided to (or not to) because. . . .
- What an insightful perspective. I hadn't thought of it in that way. What do you think?
- I'm not sure I understood the question. (Follow with reworded question to make it more natural, and if it is off base, it will be asked again with more explanation.)
- (If questions are far off base, or questioners are asking questions more to show expertise themselves, pivot.) It is interesting to [*repeat some of their words back to them, so they know they were heard*], and that reminds me of [*state what you want to say to get back on track even if there is no connection*].

A well-prepared candidate does not have a word-perfect speech ready. Showing depth of knowledge is much more important and ending the presentation with thanks to the committee members sets up the questioning in a positive manner.

Preparing the Committee Members for Proposal and Defense

At oral defense, committee members should be professional, empathetic, and tactful. Unfortunately, a few do not know this and come to the meeting like a figure skating judge ready to deduct points. Improved etiquette is possible for the Chair to encourage when the draft is sent to the committee and at the beginning of the presentation. When the draft is sent, sending an email to each member can lay out what is expected. A sample message could be:

> *Marcus is sending you his full dissertation with a request for defense in three weeks. We appreciate your time in reading his conclusions and discussions. If you find minor edits that need to be fixed, please tab them and bring it to me at or before defense. If your concerns are significant, please call me in the next two weeks so that they may be addressed when I meet with Marcus. Thank you for your support of this deserving candidate.*

By implying that major concerns should be given to the Chair in advance, if someone starts an unexpected attack at defense, it is easy to turn to the person and calmly ask why the concern was not communicated as requested. Those who enjoy springing nasty surprises do not like to be seen as not following protocol themselves. If major concerns are uncovered, the defense can be delayed without embarrassing the student or wasting the full commit-tee's time.

At the beginning of the meeting, the Chair can set the ground rules. Along with time, order, and process, it is good to turn to the candidate and say that the committee has read the paper and has had the chance to forward any questions or suggestions for major changes. Remind him or her that the committee agreed to participate because they wish to support the candidate and approve that the findings are ready for wider publication. The Chair may be speaking to the candidate, but the message is for the committee. Healthy debate and constructive suggestions are welcomed, but grandstanding is not.

Questioning at a defense can become too rote and repetitive, too petty and nitpicky, or too meaningless and off topic. This occurs when professors do not have a clear idea of how to direct a discussion by asking high-level and appropriate questions. Review of questioning for all faculty can help their teaching as well as committee work. Specifically, for a defense questions could be framed for the following purposes:

Clarifying—questions that provide more information about the facts

"Could you elaborate on that point?"
"What did you mean by the term . . . ?"

Increasing critical awareness—questions that ask for evaluation or interpreta-tion

"What are you assuming?"
"How would an opponent of this point of view respond?"

Refocusing—questions to broaden or deepen the thinking

"If this is true, what are the implications for . . . ?"
"Can you relate this to . . . ?"

Prompting—questions to focus or reframe the thinking

"Would you share how your conceptual framework was developed?"
"Could you tell us about the criteria you used to analyze theme 2?"

There are many good lists of prompts for questions available and having one as a handout for committee members can vary the questions, phrase them in nonthreatening ways, and spark members' thinking.

PUBLISHING AND PRESENTING

The final responsibility of the committee is to see that the graduate has the opportunity and encouragement to publish and present findings. There are options available for graduate students to publish the completed paper, but in many cases, it takes outside help for someone to tear apart the carefully crafted dissertation or thesis to make it ready for submission. By teaming with the new professional, the Chair or interested committee member ensures that all the effort does not become a dusty library book and instead is shared with interested audiences. The goal of the process in the end is more about creating an active researcher than graduating one.

POINTS TO CONSIDER

- Each member of the committee, especially the Chair, needs to know the expectations and responsibilities that the university, candidate, and other committee members have for the process and themselves. Assumptions lead to disappointments and more work.
- Consider the unique background of your student. Is he or she an international student? Part-time student? Entirely online student? Each of these presents challenges that must be handled professionally and with care. Ask questions and invest in your student so that what might be obstacles to completion become assets.
- Directly set out ground rules with the candidate. As Chair, the more students know when, how, and with whom to get support, the fewer stressful meetings and frantic emails will appear.
- Creating a positive culture for dissertation and thesis committees includes putting together people who are respectful enough to be encouraging of one another and the study, but also who are interested enough to ask the tough questions early.
- People who like to show their own intelligence by playing "gotcha" at a defense are not good ambassadors for the university or program, nor do they understand that the purpose of the committee is to be a gold mine of expertise rather than a gauntlet of superiority.

Chapter Four

Planning the Dissertation with the Candidate

CASE STUDY—PART 4

After getting the committee set up, Chair began meeting with Student in order to lay out their next few semesters together navigating this final scholarly study. Student presented an idea he was passionate about studying, one that he had encountered during his coursework and that he felt could change how the world views education.

His topic was extremely broad and his sample size was enormous. Student presented an argument for why the study should be done, as Chair wondered how she would tell Student the topic would not work. Chair asked what other theses or dissertations Student had read on the topic and he admitted he had read none. In fact, Student had never seen a dissertation and began peppering Chair with questions about how long the paper needed to be, how many drafts would be required, and what semester he could plan to graduate. Chair was speechless and confused.

- *How can Chair better prepare to plan the thesis or dissertation process with Student?*
- *What considerations should Chair take when saying "yes" or "no" to a potential topic?*
- *What questions should Chair be prepared to ask Student in their initial planning stages?*

While the Chair is busy building the foundation and the relationship at the beginning of the process, it is the process itself that consumes the candidate.

This is a challenge that has long been on the candidates' minds, and they come with their interpretation of what others have done that they want to emulate or avoid. The first agreement needs to be on the broad topic or field. It is surprising how often the candidate leaps immediately to the data set, pragmatic research question, or theme where they believe they already know the "right" answer. Those who did not write a thesis in a previous degree are more prone to this; not only is the process unknown, but so are the strengths of the candidate as a writer of long, complex research. Uncertainty can be just as interfering as overconfidence to starting a new project, so the role of the Chair is to *comfort the afflicted* and *afflict the comfortable*.

COMFORT THE AFFLICTED

Case in point: Peggy was anxious about her first meeting with her thesis Chair. She had worked with Dr. L in the past, and yet was not sure what would be needed at this point. She felt that she was not ready to put forward a great idea for a study. She had several ideas but could not decide what Dr. L would think of her plans.

Peggy loaded a bag with highlighted articles and tabbed books in case she needed to show that she had been thinking about her topic. At the meeting, she tried to act professional and ready, but she hoped Dr. L could not see that he lost her in his questions and suggestions with terms she had never heard. She left hoping that he did not realize what a disaster she was. Peggy called her friends in the program for advice, but there was no one to whom she could confide her worries that she would never graduate.

Candidates have many questions about what to write and how to write, yet they have reached a level of professional status in graduate school that they think they *should* know it all. Too often key questions remain unasked as candidates put forward a façade of security that leaves them blundering around the library, trying to emulate other dissertations without understanding the reasoning, or getting advice from other candidates who may be just as confused. Comfort comes from a direct set of guidelines, options for seeking help, and a feeling that ambiguity is normal in the process.

The university, college, department, professional field, and Chair all have set ideas about how to create a dissertation. A one-stop guide, either written or online, that explains style, formatting, organization, and other conventions prevents a lot of frustration from guessing and then rewriting. Providing exemplars for candidates has the benefit of providing models of the standards expected but has the limitation of candidates trying to replicate sections that are not appropriate to the new study.

Hersey and Blanchard's Situational Leadership (Hersey, Blanchard, & Johnson, 2013) sets a model for how to determine the type and amount of help the Chair may need to apply to be successful. This frame looks to the follower's maturity to determine the action of the leader. The two dimensions of this maturity are manifested in the follower's willingness and ability to accomplish the task. So, in terms of a thesis or dissertation student, one who is willing, or motivated, to write and able, or skilled, to do so needs the Chair to *delegate*. Providing criteria for success, reviewing, reading, and revising, and praising the accomplishments are these tasks. Delegating is not abdicating leadership or leaving the student to proceed alone. While it is tempting to spend little time on self-sufficient students, all candidates need reassurance at times, and writing a thesis or dissertation can be a long, lonely effort without the interaction of an interested Chair to act as sounding board.

Situational Leadership suggests that if the follower is neither willing nor able, the leader should be *directive*. It would seem that a student who does not have sufficient motivation or skills should not be continued in the program, but many hard-working students find that the dissertation or thesis is a new and difficult challenge unlike any attempted in earlier education. What may seem to be lack of motivation can be fear of failure, and skills may need to be redefined or reviewed for a research study. The Chair is directive through approving small steps, meeting more often, and providing clear and precise feedback and models.

A third type of student is one who is willing, but not able, and needs skill support and guidance from the Chair. If the Chair does not understand the student's background and classes taken, it is easy to give mixed messages that the student misinterprets. It is also necessary to do more than hand the student a source to read or model to replicate. It calls for the Chair actively *participating* in the learning. Without understanding where errors are being made or why changes are necessary, progress is uneven. However, many times the skills are sufficient, and the feeling of not being able actually is insecurity. The role of the Chair is participating by encouraging and problem solving with the candidate through the process.

A graduate student who is able, but not willing, is likely hiding fears as well. This person would rather be seen as belligerent or uncooperative than test his or her abilities. Explaining and persuading, or *selling*, is the task of the Chair. It is easier to work with this student with a chip on the shoulder when the Chair frames the antagonism as the student's self-protection. Keeping empathy with all types of students takes patience, emotional intelligence, and persistence.

The Chair should directly and repeatedly remind all candidates that there are multiple avenues for getting help. Writing centers, tutors, editors, research librarians, and peer support can all be very valuable. Candidates may not have required help in earlier writing efforts, so they need encouragement to utilize the resources available. Smart people too often believe that getting assistance is equated to failure or lack of knowledge; in actuality, wisdom is knowing when to use the knowledge of others. When approaching outside help, the candidate should keep the Chair in the conversation. Without ongoing communication, usefulness of the source may be superficial or misguided, which undermines the benefits of time invested.

AFFLICT THE COMFORTABLE

> ***Case in point:*** *Marty set up an initial meeting with his Chair, Dr. P. He had been getting ready for this day for years, when he could finally put his ideas into action as his dissertation. Carefully, he laid out his plan to Dr. P, showing his extensive list of sources he had read and was going to read, and the clear reasons the study should be done.*
>
> *With shock, he heard Dr. P say that he could not do the study. She pointed out fallacies in his thinking, and said he was basing his work on biases and assumptions. She tried to get him to limit his study so that it was exploratory rather than cause and effect. Marty thought her ideas washed out the beauty of his plan, and he left the meeting ready to find friends who would commiserate. He hoped that he would find the right words to persuade Dr. P next time.*

Some candidates come to the study phase of their program brimming with enthusiasm for a broad, general, or large study that would take them years to get the expertise to do, more years to collect the data, and maybe never get to useful conclusions. Others have a tiny pet project that does not come up to the standard of a thesis or dissertation. Listening to the initial idea can be tiring for the Chair, but it may be the most important time in the whole process. This is when the Chair needs to be realistic with the student about what should and can be done, and then inspiring about his or her ability and the value of doing well.

Most candidates bring the Chair an initial idea that was sparked by a problem uncovered in their reading, experience, or coursework. As the Chair is listening to the background and value in the story of the initial idea, the focus is probably rambling. An interesting task is to try to boil down the idea into a tentative or working research question. Doing that points to the parts of the idea that are missing, vague, or grandiose. Usually one of two patterns emerges.

The first is an idea that is deeply philosophical, has great consequences if it could be answered, but is thin in how to specifically create a study out of it. The second is practical, with the question, the instrument, the participants, and the methods mostly in place but of local or immediate interest.

What do they have in common? The creators of either type of idea have a strong aversion to the Chair telling them no and a vocal confidence that the idea is viable. Overconfidence may be real as it stems from past successes, or a masquerade as it is covering for shortcomings. The Chair's intention at this point is not to unravel the motivation, but to move to a crisp, viable study idea. To get through the unrealistic or messy components, a gentle and unswayable "no" is predominantly the correct response to a first idea. Either it will motivate the student to dig deeper and correct the flaws to convince the Chair, or it saves the student weeks or months of working toward a goal that has too many faults to sustain.

In *QBQ!* (2012), Miller describes the idea of the question behind the question. A great study seeks this deeper, focused idea. To unearth a true research question, the Chair can begin by asking, "What do you really want to know?" Depending on the conversation to that point, emphasis could be, "What do *you* really want to know," "*What* do you really want to know," or even, "What do you *really* want to know?"

In any case, what is being discussed is finding the sweet spot of a study that the candidate has the passion to study, the objective perspective to evaluate, and the expertise to conduct. The topic needs to be narrowed to a practical timeframe and scope, and have a focus on uncovering new, meaningful conclusions. Candidates often leave the initial meeting with more questions than when they arrived, but with a direction on what needs to be refined to create the purpose statement and research question. Once those are developed, the method, research site availability, and writing process can provide benchmarks for upcoming steps.

Start with why, then what and how. It would be nice if every student came to the initial meeting with the Chair having a clear, reasonable idea around which to build a study. A large percentage get to that point still wandering around and not ready to commit to a topic. They talk about having many things they would like to study and being afraid to choose the wrong one. They wonder if the ideas they have were already completed by other dissertations somewhere. They went through their classes thinking a great idea would appear magically, and it never happened.

One way a Chair can move toward commitment is to ask students what they see themselves doing in five years. In what specialty would they like to be the area, national, or even international expert? A vision of their own use for the learning, rather than the weight of a huge and unfamiliar assignment, should guide the thinking.

There are many research books for students that address choosing a topic. If the student is paralyzed at this point, these may be too specific to unfreeze them. General motivational books like *Influencer* (Grenny, Patterson, Maxfield, McMillan, & Switzler, 2013) can inspire a person to see the power one can have to make a difference. This power is not figuring out the grandest study, or being the best writer alive, but in matching the will to inspect a problem and to a method that systematically moves a specific question a bit closer to solution.

A good book for a student who cannot commit to a topic is Sinek's (2009) *Start with Why.* Even though this volume was written for business leaders, the framework, philosophy, and stories are easy to translate into dissertation/

thesis creation. Giving a copy of this to a student not only helps focus thinking; it gives the message that the Chair looks upon the student as a leader with the potential to use this opportunity to answer great questions and solve real issues.

CRITERIA TO SET AS GROUND RULES

Beginning with a plain understanding of what is expected and what can be expected by the other benefits both student and Chair. Each situation calls for reading verbal and nonverbal signals but having a common set of procedures and documented records protects faculty from students feeling they are being treated capriciously. By spelling out how the upcoming steps will be handled preempts manipulation and posturing. Agreeing upon communication patterns as well as the shape and scope of the study can help avoid common conflicts.

Managing both the logical sequence of tasks while upholding an ethical, empathetic relationship is easier if started with direct attention to ground rules. Basic interpersonal agreements can help prevent misunderstandings, and agreements about the product ensures quality. All of the following questions are not necessary to be articulated but thinking about these components can help leave less to assumption.

Setting Up Communication

1. How often should the candidate and Chair meet? Who initiates the meetings?
2. Which kinds of questions should be referred to the Chair, and what questions go to other sources first?
3. When should drafts be presented for reading?
4. How long should the candidate wait for feedback before checking with the Chair?
5. What pet peeves upset the other person? What subjects are taboo? What is nonnegotiable?
6. What is the process if there is a personality conflict, major difference of opinion, or neglect?

Depth of the Topic

1. Is the purpose of the study meaningful; does it add to understanding?
2. Are there prospective new perspectives or perceptions that are unique and not readily available in literature?

3. Does the candidate have the background and interest to see this clearly and in a new light? Does he or she have ethical access to the data?
4. Is there a reasonable theory or conceptual framework that logically sets the foundation for the study?
5. Will the proposed study observe a large enough sample to generalize?

Breadth of the Study

1. Does the research question have academic merit and broad significance to generalize to a broader field?
2. Is there a tentative map or outline of the literature review? What is crucial and what is unnecessary to understand and undergird the new research?
3. Is the research question aligned to method?
4. Are terms, scope, participants, and variables neither too narrow nor too ambitious?

Length of Time and Manuscript

1. What is the overall outline of the chapters and topics for a study?
2. How will literature be mapped to make sense?
3. Is data available in a timely manner?
4. Can it result in a timely graduation date?
5. Will the candidate emerge as an expert in the field?

> ***Case in point:*** *Sara had been calling or emailing Dr. I at least three or four times a week. The questions were not long, but the answers could be found in basic texts and in other studies from the same department. She was not getting the hints that she was asking for information that was readily available with little effort. When she turned in a draft, she expected feedback within 24 hours. Delaying replies meant that messages were going to the department office staff, asking if Dr. I was all right as she was not getting answers to her messages.*
>
> *Dr. I asked Sara to come in for a meeting. After answering all Sara's current questions, Dr. I reminded her that there was a limit to what a student should expect from a Chair. With all the other responsibilities that would come later in the process, basic questions would be more efficiently looked up, and a draft that took six weeks to write deserved more than six hours to be read. Sara cried, feeling that Dr. I did not understand the pressures she was under to graduate. Dr. I kindly smiled and firmly gave Sara a list of articles, books, and dissertations that she might find helpful.*

Requiring students to rent or purchase books about the method for their study, literature reviews, and about researching in their field gives students security on solid, approved sources of help that an online search does not provide. Candidates believe that they know how to write in the style guide, but always have new issues not previously encountered.

So, for example, a candidate conducting qualitative education research could be required to purchase the *APA Manual* (2010), Creswell's (2015) research text, Krathwohl and Smithe's (2005) proposal book, and Savin-Baden and Major's (2012) qualitative manual. While this is not the extent of the books and articles needed, having a common set of guides allows the Chair to refer to specific pages and sections and gives the student a direction to find answers independently.

IMPACT OF THE METHOD ON THE JOURNEY

Setting forth ground rules, time lines, and benchmarks with the student takes different paths based upon the methodology. Choosing the best method for a dissertation or thesis is directly dependent upon the research question and the data available, but the skills and knowledge of the candidate can also be the determining factor.

Occasionally, a student may express interest for a feasible study, only to discover well into the process that the skills or knowledge to complete the method are lacking. At that point the Chair is faced with redesigning the study, which the student will resist because previous work must be redone, or with teaching the skills the student is lacking, which the Chair should resist; it is time consuming and results in a shaky study when the foundation is not deep and broad. If knowledge of the method is sound, but the candidate does not demonstrate the disposition or writing preferences necessary for the method, there will be issues with procrastination or unsuccessful drafts.

> ***Case in point.*** *Barry was in charge of a new program over the last two years. Much data had been collected on the program that had not been analyzed to evaluate whether the objectives of the program were being met. Gleefully, he brought the data sets to Dr. O, and they settled on the research questions, sub-questions, and statistical analysis to be run.*
>
> *Barry's proposal went well, but when the data were analyzed, Dr. O returned it immediately. There were inaccuracies that made results wrong as well. Barry laughed and said that when he balanced his budget he worried about the dollars and let the pennies take care of themselves. It took months of working with professors to get the data to be correct for interpretation.*
>
> *Barry was disillusioned that his data did not turn into a quick, easy study, and his next draft included generalizations that could not be supported and cause and effect that was not evident. When this was explained, Barry threw a stapler across the office so hard it left a dent in the wall. Eventually, his final defense was clean and precise, painfully brief, and just enough to pass committee review. Barry had not loved his topic or the method, and so setbacks were inevitable.*

Someone like Barry, who gets frustrated when working with tables and lacks joy when analyzing statistics, should be counseled not to undertake quantitative work. Also, candidates who have trouble with telling a rich, deep story should not take on qualitative. It is not what is on their transcript that indicates the best fit.

Students may successfully take classes in qualitative, quantitative, and mixed methods—engaging as a learner without understanding what it takes to be the investigator. The Chair is looking for the aptitude for the candidate to carry out the research with minimal input from professors. This can be found by talking with the candidates about how they like to write, how they process information, and what attracts them to investigation. Reading what the student wrote in prior classes or degrees also can be very helpful in matching the student to the method they will appreciate over the long process.

Considerations for Undertaking Quantitative Research

Quantitative work takes logic and precision. Students sometimes think they need to be great at math and science to do well, but computer assisted analysis eliminates the crunching of numbers. What is needed is understanding in setting up the data to discover significance without attributing results to faulty data collection or overgeneralization.

This is not the method for someone who thinks they know the result before they begin and are only looking for numerical proof to back up their assumptions. Candidates who thrive in quantitative study have a narrow focus in a broader field of research, patience for minutiae, and the willingness to accept the limits of what the analysis uncovers. They can make interpretation from charts, tables, and graphs, and they have the skills to collect and analyze data systematically.

Ground Rules for Quantitative Research

There are specific agreements that the Chair should make clear upon setting up a quantitative study. The following must be clear:

- If using archived or retrospective data, it must either be publicly available or the candidate must have ethical access to it. This can be a problem if students have access to data in the workplace, but not to do research on it. Special education teachers, for example, often believe they may use the information they have to work with their students, but these are legal documents that cannot be reported without strong IRB oversight—if access is granted at all.

- If creating an instrument, it must be thoroughly piloted for reliability and validity. Some students put together a survey or other instrument and are surprised that the results are unusable because significance does not show up. Without documenting steps in creating the instrument and citing experts in instrument creation, it is difficult to get others to have any confidence in the work.
- If utilizing another's instrument, permission must be gained, and any small changes made carefully noted.
- The study must be a fresh look at the data, and not have the feel of repeating information that is already available, or "new wine in old bottles."
- Measures, alpha levels, effect size, etc. are set before collecting data and not manipulated during analysis to get the desired results.
- All possible outcomes should be discussed early, and a plan B arranged for partial or muddy data.

Work on a quantitative study is heaviest between the initial meeting and the proposal of the study to the committee. Making sure the study is neither too large nor too tiny, and that it has a meaningful whole rather than a string of small data bits, are guidance that the Chair controls throughout.

Considerations for Undertaking Qualitative Research

Qualitative studies do not take as much of a Chair's time before proposal but become intense in the implementation of data collection and analysis. The qualitative researcher must be comfortable in flying without a net; the data can take the research in new and unexpected directions. This realization is often late in the study when the student is tired and does not want to engage in new literature review. Starting with the idea that the work is exploratory (and that any literature reviewed before proposal is foundational only) helps the student understand why it seemed that completing the proposal was quick and getting to defense overwhelming.

Ground Rules for Qualitative Research

Mapping the general areas of the study and creating a protocol of questions assists the Chair and student to be of the same mind about the direction and focus of the study. Knowing what can be changed along the way and what remains unchanged is especially important for the novice qualitative researcher.

- Understand that there will be much ambiguity in the earlier stages that will not be resolved until coding is done.

- Articulate all the steps by careful documentation. Use of field notes should be started as soon as the topic is decided so there is no reliance on fallible memory.
- Starting with a self-reflection of the role of the researcher and all possible biases brought to the research will raise awareness of what to avoid or point out.
- Tone and voice of the author should be set. Is the use of first person acceptable rather than "the researcher"?

Considerations for Mixed Method Research

Many graduate students are drawn to a mixed method study; it shows off all the skills they have learned and seems to be the broadest way to be sure to uncover significant results. "If one measure is good two is better" is a deceptive mindset. Concurrent data collection can make triangulation problematic, so sequential exploratory or explanatory design may be easier for the Chair to direct and the student to complete.

Ground Rules for Mixed Method Research

- Each section of the study should have a deliberate purpose that is different from other sections.
- The student needs to be expert in all methods undertaken as well as how to make sense of data between sections and reconcile differences uncovered.
- If qualitative or quantitative alone answers the question, mixed method should be abandoned for expediency.

Other Considerations in Method

There are other forms of dissertations and theses that do not fit a pure quantitative or qualitative route. For example, an English major may present a portfolio of original works interspersed with autoethnography and seeking themes toward which they gravitate as an author. Program evaluation is another design that has both qualitative and quantitative strengths to measure the quality of an organization or initiative. Creating the method from an evaluation standpoint is often valuable for a student who will enter a career where such decision making is vital.

> *Case in point: Debra was the head of a residence school for children with special needs. While there was some data to measure success of the program, much was too confidential for public analysis. Dr. K suggested that Debra engage in objectives-based evaluation, and Debra found a framework that was adaptable to create her measures. When she completed, Debra's work not only had insights and suggestions for the future of the school, but a wider audience*

in ways to analyze data systematically and objectively from many sensitive sources.

Ground Rules for Unique Studies

There is no reason to create a unique method when a tried-and-true methodology works. Creating an out-of-the-box method for answering a research question is the last resort. There is comfort in having many examples at hand, and so even unique studies need to have patterns that compare and contrast to established methods.

- While it takes a maverick to establish a unique research design, each step needs to be approved to keep the legitimacy of the work. Going too far afield may mean major revisions or unaccepted defense.
- Sometimes what seems to be a unique design is a basic method described in a unique way. In this case, leaning on the established method for the study, then explaining the creative innovation, provides the outline of a respected design.

A Chinese philosopher noted that a journey of a thousand miles begins with a single step. Thoughtful preplanning supported with documents sets the pattern for the future steps. Starting a journey without a map is either foolish or frustrating, and the map of the next steps as well as the ground rules for the candidate should be copied for each to use in future work together. As the study grows toward its final form, it can be helpful to return to the initial meeting documents to see what the candidate really wants to know, why the study will add to the expertise of the student and field, and how to keep to the basic agreements in difficult times.

POINTS TO CONSIDER

- Remember what it was like to start your first real research study, and how many misunderstandings and assumptions had to be shed before the work was successful.
- Choose the Chair's roles of directing, teaching, coaching, and delegating based upon the student's potential to be willing and able to complete the task.
- Choosing a methodology is a process that should take deliberation and time, but not too much deliberation and time. That is, ensure that the student has the capacity to build a research study. When you see weaknesses, step in and encourage the student to build his or her research methodology toolbox.

- The tipping point between discussing and undertaking a thesis or dissertation is the Chair and candidate agreeing on the specific purpose and research question and deciding upon the method, instrument, and participants that will answer that purpose and question.
- Written outlines or other forms of organization should be in the student's hands to accurately portray the depth, breadth, sometimes length, and other crucial benchmarks of what is in and what is beyond the study.

Chapter Five

Feedback and Failure

CASE STUDY—PART 5

Chair and Student finally agreed on an appropriate topic and Student was set to begin working on his first few drafts and the initial design of his study. Student, who had excelled at coursework, sent an email attaching his first draft and Chair diligently spent more than five days reading and editing the work. The conceptual framework of the study was solid, but the literature review needed more resources and the proposed method needed a few extra steps.

Chair and Student met to discuss the feedback and it became apparent that Student was not handling seeing so many suggestions for changes in his paper. Student grew silent and hung his head in dismay. He explained how much time he had invested in this draft and really thought he was ready to head to his proposal meeting. Chair disagreed and noted that Student had a lot of work left to do before his study could be approved. Student looked at Chair and bluntly stated, "I'm such a failure. I don't think I can get this done. And I don't know if I want to anymore."

- *What considerations should Chair think about when providing feedback to Student?*
- *How can Chairs help accomplished students face critical feedback?*
- *When Student noted that he felt like a "failure," how best could Chair respond?*

Graduate students are generally accomplished and driven individuals. After all, in order to get to the stage of writing a thesis or dissertation, a student must have attained admission to graduate school, accumulated a certain number of credit hours, and generally have passed some sort of comprehensive exam. Many balance full-time jobs, families, and homework throughout the course of multiple years.

Despite the multitude of responsibilities faced by graduate students, many are accustomed to receiving positive feedback and praise for work produced in the classroom. When the thesis or dissertation stage hits, the student may be unprepared for the multiple phases of feedback and editing required to get to completion.

In addition, a lot of feedback provided by Chairs and committee members is critical in nature; that is, rather than pointing out the strengths of a student's writing, there may only be time to point out the weaknesses and areas that need improvement. This type of feedback can leave a once accomplished student wondering if he or she is even capable of writing a large academic production like a thesis or dissertation. The Chair's role in this is integral—helping a graduate student understand the nature and purpose of feedback and to learn to take critical feedback as a means to grow as an academic.

SETTING UP STUDENT/CHAIR COMMUNICATION

College faculty each have a strong appreciation for our own dissertation Chair and carry that into our work with students today. However, most concur that learning how to communicate with a Chair, often someone who works as a part- or full-time faculty member at a university, can be challenging for a working graduate student.

> **Case in point:** *Joan was a very busy professional who wrote each weekend. When she finished a chapter, she would email it to Dr. W. Joan would wait weeks and would call him to see if he had been able to look at her draft. Dr. W replied that he had not received it or was too busy to read it. This happened repeatedly. Knowing his feedback was not going to be consistent or easy to get, Joan contacted a long-time mentor who was able to help with drafts.*

When graduates like Joan become professors, they vow to treat students differently. They may become overly conscientious of student needs. As soon as they see a message from a student, they immediately acknowledge receipt. If it requires a short answer, they take care of the question immediately. Because of their own Chair's lack of responsiveness and the uneasiness of feeling inadequate or just not knowing what to do, they compensate because they never want a student to feel the same.

Graduate students have had classes from numerous professors, and they are well aware of different expectations and requirements in the classes. Having a single Chair of the thesis or dissertation with one-on-one guidance is new. Getting to know one another is the first step to a successful relationship.

As a Chair, ask a lot of questions about work, family, growing up, and the research interests of the student in order to understand the person with whom you will be working. When things get tense, this type of familiarity can help put aside the paper and talk about life. Developing a trusting relationship with the student matters to their success and yours. Having a list of rules is not necessary, but it may be helpful to have a working checklist to use when talking about the mutual needs for communication in a successful thesis or dissertation relationship. Some questions that might be included on a communication checklist could be:

- When would you like to meet? On a regular basis? Or when you are at a place in your writing when you need support?
- Do you prefer email, texts, or phone calls?
- Are you comfortable with online collaboration?
- If meeting during office hours, what days and times work the best?
- Since we are meeting after hours, I prefer to meet in a public place. What would work for you?
- What is a draft in your eyes? How well developed should it be?
- How much time are you willing to wait for feedback? What is reasonable for you?
- When you face challenges or a problem, how do you usually handle stress?
- What type of support system do you have now to walk with you through this process? Family? Friends? Coworkers?
- What is your goal after graduation and this process is done?
- What do you want me to know about you as a person to help me understand our relationship better?
- Is there anything in particular you expect from me?

HELPING STUDENTS UNDERSTAND
THE TIMING OF THE PROCESS

Many Chairs have stories about the student who sent a revised draft on Thursday evening and then called the office Friday morning waiting on feedback. Students sometimes have very unrealistic expectations, and it is important to tell them the parameters at the very beginning of the process.

> **Case in point:** *Charles had stepped out of the program for a short amount of time due to medical issues. He contacted Dr. E when he was feeling well and met with her three times in one semester, but without progress on his part. The student did not have any contact with Dr. E for another two years.*

> *Out of the blue, Charles sent Dr. E an email that said, "I would like to meet next Wednesday to talk about how you can help me finish my dissertation and graduate in December." She wrote back simply that he would not be able to finish by December graduation, but she would like to meet with him and help him work on his dissertation. Dr. E heard nothing further. However, Charles complained to the department chair, who gave him the same information. Charles has not been heard from since, but rumor has it that he has joined another doctoral program.*

It is not uncommon for students like Charles to appear, disappear, and reappear during their time at a university. However, sometimes students are simply unaware of the institutional demands behind a thesis or dissertation, mainly that there are processes and protocols that need to be followed. For most, if not all students, the thesis or dissertation is not a one-semester journey. It takes multiple semesters and sometimes many years to complete. Some students do not understand the nature of research, the diligence of data collection, or the actual purpose of thesis or dissertation itself, which, in turn, causes unrealistic expectations as to how soon completion can occur. Throughout their course of studies, students should have opportunities to look at and study published theses or dissertations to understand how complex and difficult one can be to complete. It is with familiarity that an understanding of the process can be explained clearly and the student's assumption that it's "just another term paper" can quickly fade.

THE CHAIR'S WORKLOAD

Most tenured professors have the requirement of teaching, research, and service. On some campuses, the thesis or dissertation load falls under teaching, while on other campuses it might be considered research or service. Regardless of where the actual workload of the thesis or dissertation falls on one's rank and tenure file, generally serving as a Chair is not one's only job on campus. Finding a sane balance in managing an academic workload including teaching, service, and research is a sensitive area for most academics. Depending on your load with other assignments, it is important to consider the time you can devote to your role as a Chair. It is imperative that students come first—that is, regardless of the workload of the Chair, the student should receive prompt attention in a timely manner. What works in the classroom does not always work on a thesis or dissertation committee, so one must also display an aptitude and flexibility for learning.

Chairing a dissertation involves learning on the part of both the student and the Chair. No two dissertations are alike, and it is crucial to understand that besides meeting with the student, one probably needs to set aside time to study the proposed methodology and research topic in order to be able to give the student the guidance needed to be successful.

One of our colleagues indicated that he sees each student research committee on which he serves as the equivalent to teaching a three-credit-hour course. It takes a tremendous amount of time to serve students well, but this service also must come with boundaries. Students should not expect Chairs to answer phone calls or emails at inappropriate times or in an unreasonable timeframe. Chairs should also not be subject to unprofessional conduct by students, regardless of how frustrating the relationship or situation may become. While students are the priority, so, too, is the well-being of the Chair. While the Chair should be responsible for learning about the topic, engaging alongside the student in the research planning, and assisting with reviewing drafts of work, the ownership of the work needed should fall on the student's shoulders.

It is important not to underestimate the amount of administrative work required in chairing a thesis or dissertation. Beyond reading drafts and conferring with the student, you are also expected to adhere to a multitude of institutional time lines and guidelines. It is helpful when you accept a committee assignment to immediately ask for any institutional manuals, checklists, time lines, and forms. Very often you will be responsible for collecting signatures, adhering to strict guidelines, and securing copies of administrative paperwork. Oversights in this area can cause delays for the student and may, in fact, cause a student to miss important deadlines.

TEARS AND FEARS

Writing a dissertation can be a daunting challenge. The unfamiliar format of a thesis or dissertation and the rigor of writing can easily feel overwhelming to students. It is not uncommon for students to begin to question their intellectual ability as a result of being overwhelmed. Self-doubt can begin to creep in slowly and unless managed, can throw a student completely off course. Students begin to realize that the coursework they took to get to this point pales in comparison of rigor and workload. The work is now independent, students are left to be the experts, and they question their own ability to judge scholarly work. Students feel inadequate when the work they are doing includes a level of challenge that they have never faced before in their graduate program. Some, if not all, will experience fatigue and failure at some point in the process.

Helping students understand that they need to rely upon you for guidance is important. The necessity of your leadership and support is critical to your student during the research and writing process. You may need to have a conversation about how the student needs more background on his or her topic, or the methodology or approach needs to be adjusted. Even these small conversations can leave a student wondering if the task is worth the effort. Paying attention to the student's challenges and giving your support and direction will help the student maintain the momentum that he or she needs.

Moreover, helping the student understand that the research he or she is uncovering is something new and not always similar to what we read in textbooks can help the student understand that the process may feel like walking in the wilderness. Students are the experts on their topic, but doing the research will stretch that knowledge further, helping them develop more skills and certainly a deeper understanding of their topic. It is our role to help the student relax, be comfortable with the ambiguity of not knowing every-thing.

CRITICAL FEEDBACK OR COACHING?

Helping students to understand the role and purpose of feedback from the very beginning of the Chair/student relationship is important for overall success. Students need to know that, at times, the written and verbal feedback received during the thesis or dissertation process will be hard to hear and difficult to digest. Some feedback will be harsh, feel personal, and may even cause the student to consider quitting the journey. Therefore it is important to prepare the student for the type of feedback he or she will receive during the thesis or dissertation process.

Share your critique philosophy with the student and let him or her know that criticism without support is not appropriate. That is, as you share feedback about what the student may need to change, edit, or redo, also provide advice to help the student and give the student the direction and resources to help make that change. For example, simply telling a student that the methodology section in the paper is weak is not helpful. Telling a student that the methodology section needs more development and giving very specific suggestions, even examples of similar studies, can turn the critique into meaningful coaching. Encourage the student to look at models of others' writing and to find inspiration and direction from that process. Let the student know that all researchers go through multiple drafts of each section of a study before it finally reaches a point suitable for publication.

Preparing the student to handle critical feedback is important, but professors have to realize that as Chairs, they are not always the experts at allowing students to process and perhaps disagree with feedback. Chairs need to be open to discussing why they provided certain feedback and to help the student understand what the intent was as well. Having an honest discussion between student and Chair about student concerns with the feedback increases the likelihood of overall agreement between both parties while also building trust in the relationship.

Avoiding feedback is also not good practice for a Chair. No paper is going to arrive perfect, and it is the mentoring role to help the student advance in the profession by doing quality work. Some Chairs struggle with the balance between providing feedback and editing a student's paper. This is a difficult position to balance, but one that must be clearly established by the Chair. Theses and dissertations are independent scholarly work that is intellectually demanding by design. By not receiving substantive feedback, a student can be left wondering about the quality or worthiness of the work being produced. Thus, be sure to take the time to carefully read and critique the substance of the study in front of you.

SHOULDN'T THE STUDENT ALREADY KNOW THIS?

Sometimes the Chair wonders, "Shouldn't graduate students know how to do this? Didn't they learn this in their 'Introduction to Research' course?" Typically, the answer to this is both yes and no. Students have sometimes completed anywhere from 60 to 100 credit hours over the span of several years. What may have been learned in the context of the classroom may have long been forgotten or unclear as to how the concepts apply to the thesis or dissertation process.

> ***Case in point:*** *Dr. P scrolled down what Jessie called her proposal. It was a Frankenstein's monster of a paper with the logic of one chapter not matching the premise of the next. It was clear that Jessie had used the university writing center to smooth her usual choppy style into more professional prose, but the organization seemed patched together from different professors' classes. Dr. P prepared an outline template for Jessie to fill in and highlighted the paragraphs that matched the purpose of the study to become the starting point for revision.*

Students need guidance to put the puzzle together even though they probably actually know most of the pieces. Again, patience is a virtue here. Directing students to texts, articles, and resources to refresh their memory or to teach new concepts is an important Chair skill. Over time, each will probably build a regular set of resources toward which to readily point new students.

Teaching students during the thesis or dissertation process to become scholarly writers is often taken for granted, but it is an integral part of the process. Surprisingly, many graduate students do not write or think like scholars (Caffarella & Barnett, 2000). These researchers found that students used three distinct strategies in approaching their written work: planning, revising, and mixed strategies. While the authors acknowledged that these are important, none are either a necessary or sufficient condition for writing success.

Instead, both "think, then write" strategies and "think while writing" strategies have utility in the context of academic writing. That is, students need to write, extensively, to experience the flow and style of academic writing. Students need to understand and experience the depth of thought necessary to analyze ideas and synthesize scholarly writings. Planning and revising are important but are simply steps to accomplish the main goal of the thoughtful writing itself. The authors did admit, however, that no one form of writing will be suitable for all students. They advise that different instructional supports be shared, and students be allowed to choose those that fitted their needs.

Peer feedback can be a strong tool to use in order to build a student's capacity both to understand how feedback is generated, but also how to accept feedback from others. Caffarella and Barnett also studied how students learned to accept feedback in a peer setting. In all, students were anxious to see if their feedback helped the peer, and it built confidence when they read the papers of others and were able to compare the work to their own writing ability. Students in writing groups who share feedback will gain tremendous skills toward becoming scholarly writers. The feedback from their doctoral or thesis Chair will likely be welcomed rather than a cause for dismay.

POINTS TO CONSIDER

- Have regular meetings and get to know the student. Do this in a public place such as the student union, the local coffee shop, or a restaurant. Not only will the public meeting spot protect the integrity of the meeting, it will also allow the student to relax as you discuss scholarship and progress.
- Be aware of the signs of depression in students and know where they can find help on campus. If a student is unresponsive to your emails and making little progress, attempt to reach the student to check on his or her well-being during the process. Demonstrate that the student's well-being is a priority above all other tasks at hand.
- Remind students that they have a life beyond their degree and need to balance the needs of their family, their health, and their graduate program. Encourage these relationships. Give students permission to go to a movie, take a vacation, or simply take the weekend off from writing. Sometimes students need this direction from Chairs in order to feel that they are not evading writing or ignoring responsibilities.

- Encourage students to write and critique each other's writing. The input from other students is often less threatening and less traumatic to read. In addition, it allows another set of eyes, beyond your own, to read the paper and look for holes or weaknesses. Value this input.
- Coach; do not criticize. Realize the distinction in your tone, word choice, and inflection. Reread your responses to students and imagine what the student reads when the response is received.
- Advisors or Chairs need to prepare for meetings with students. Be sure you have read the student's submitted work, questions, and other comments before meeting with the student. It is quite unprofessional to show up to a student meeting with no background on what the student wants to discuss and may actually cause the student to lose trust in your leadership.
- Teach students to be scholars in their thinking and their writing. Remind students of this—that your questions and critiques are to make them stronger scholars, not to make them weak humans. Encourage creativity, well-read responses, and scholarly dialogue. Give students a chance to practice talking through important concepts with you during the dissertation or thesis process.

Chapter Six

The Ambiguity and Loneliness of the Graduate Student

CASE STUDY—PART 6

Student was working diligently on his data collection and multiple drafts of his study. Student had been an excellent performer in his graduate school classes, so he assumed that writing this final paper would be a pretty easy task to complete.

He was wrong.

Self-doubt started to creep in. He missed talking through issues with his classmates. He envied his fellow students who were still able to sit in class and converse about readings and ponder case studies. His connections with professors started to feel distant. His numerous long evenings in front of his computer screen caused him to feel exhausted at work the next day. His kids started to ask when he would be done with his project.

Student's health began to decline as well. Prior to taking on his dissertation, Student had eaten a balanced diet and exercised daily. He now found himself prioritizing his research over time in the gym and eating burgers and fries on his way to and from the library. There would always be time to focus on himself after the defense, right? He convinced himself that this would soon pass, and he could get back to his "regular" life soon enough. What was most important was finishing the task.

- *How can Chair emphasize the importance of well-being to Student?*
- *What strategies can Chair share with Student to maintain a balance during this difficult time?*

- *What red flags should Chair watch for to indicate that Student might need some additional help or resources to help deal with personal or health issues?*

While much of this book deals with how to help a student complete the thesis or dissertation, we must acknowledge that some students simply will not complete the work to earn their degree. As Chairs, we most likely want our students to complete their thesis or dissertation and graduate. To graduate is important, but even more important is the overall growth and success of the student.

Students invest a significant amount of time and money to receive an advanced degree. According to the Council of Graduate Schools, a seven-year study indicates that the average completion rate is approximately 50%. Most students who exit doctoral programs do so before reaching the dissertation stage (Miller, 2009). Thus, odds are that you will work with students who never finish their graduate program. They may face personal obstacles, financial issues, professional demands, or may simply just want to quit. Whatever the reason, it is important to understand that providing students with tools to aid completion is one strategy to help mitigate qualified students from leaving the graduate process.

Thesis and dissertation writers often have difficulty handling ambiguity. They start comparing themselves to other students, talking about the weaknesses of their own study, and wondering if the reward will truly be worth the treacherousness of the journey. Remind students that this is not a race and getting into a race only leads to poor-quality work. Each thesis and dissertation path is individual. Theses and dissertations are intellectually demanding by design. The requirement testing a student's ability to conduct independent scholarly work and formulate conclusions is the ticket to earning a degree.

To better equip a student to avoid drowning in ambiguity, we propose equipping students with as many tools as possible. That is, the more guidance you can provide on what a thesis or dissertation looks like, reads like, and should accomplish, the less swimming and treading water the student will do.

THE MENTAL HEALTH CRISIS AMONG
GRADUATE STUDENTS

Navigating graduate school can be challenging, even for the best students. One issue that has recently been brought to the forefront in the United States is what is deemed to be the "mental health crisis" among graduate students. A 2018 report in *Inside Higher Ed* noted that graduate school students are more susceptible to mental illness, noting that "This is largely due to social isolation, the often-abstract nature of the work and feelings of inadequacy—not to mention the slim tenure-track job market" (Flaherty, 2018, para. 1). Graduate students were more likely to experience anxiety, depression, and poor work-life balance.

One interesting finding the study reported on was the discovery that many students do not believe that their mentor provides "adequate mentorship" (para. 10). In fact, half of the respondents noted that their advisors were not assets to their careers or that they did not feel valued by their mentor (para. 11). Thus, a strong Chair/student relationship can be one factor in helping a student reduce anxiety and lessen depression throughout the graduate school relationship.

Imposter Syndrome

A recent development in the field of psychology has been the emergence of "imposter syndrome," or what is defined as "the idea that you've only succeeded due to luck, and not because of your talent or qualifications" (Abrams, 2018, para 3). Graduate students are often plagued with this because they are constantly challenged and sometimes left wondering if they have any original thoughts or ideas of their own. They begin to question whether their achievement in graduate school has been because of luck or some sort of oversight on the part of the institution. Psychologist Valerie Young identified five different types of imposter syndrome; we have added our thoughts on how we see this emerge in the lives of graduate students:

1. Perfectionists—those whose work is never good enough, even when it is exceptional.
2. Experts—those who must know every detail about a topic before moving forward with a project. For graduate students this sometimes leads to earning additional degrees or taking coursework just to be sure the student understands every aspect of a concept.
3. Natural Genius—those who have not had to work hard to achieve. When faced with a new challenge or unanticipated obstacle, these students tend to wonder if they are really as smart as they seem.
4. Soloists—those who seek to accomplish everything alone. Graduate students who do this tend to reject the input of others for fear that it will diminish their contribution to a study or will limit their understanding. These students do not like to ask for help because it means they might actually be a failure simply for asking.
5. Supermen (or Superwomen)—those who push themselves harder than everyone else to prove they are not a fraud. Graduate students who do this often balance too many things at once, neglect well-being, and burn out quickly.

Helping students cope with imposter syndrome can be a challenging process. One of the common strategies suggested to help students suffering from this is to encourage the student to articulate his or her feelings (with you or someone else they trust). Once acknowledged, it can be easier to overcome the internal doubts and fears and accept the reality of achievement and success.

It is possible that imposter syndrome may completely derail a student; after all, if one feels like a fraud, it is difficult to defend one's work confidently. It is not your job to counsel the student to wellness or to solve the student's internal battles, but an awareness that this is a common struggle for high-achieving graduate students can help you prepare feedback in a reaffirming fashion and in a way that affirms your confidence in the student's abilities.

Loneliness

Sometimes finding a partner who is also writing makes the task more bearable. Setting up those regular meetings at the library or coffee shop eliminates the loneliness of writing and gives the students someone to talk to about their writing. Talking through a research project can help a scholar identify holes, gaps, and questions. Having a regular partner to work with also creates accountability and can make it easier to focus attention on what needs to be completed.

Foss and Waters (2007) suggest that if a faculty member or another graduate student is not available, locate someone who does not know a lot about research or your fields of study. These people can be an outstanding choice as a partner in a conceptual conversation because they ask naïve or silly questions during the conversation and these questions can force the student to think concretely about the level of understanding required to articulate his or her own study.

In addition, having an outside person, someone completely uninvolved in the research topic, can help a writer identify errors, passages that need more clarity, and sections that need further clarification. Encourage your student to find a writing group, whether it be with other graduate students or writers in the community in which they live. If there isn't a writing group available, consider forming groups of your advisees or students or encouraging students to start a group on their own.

Writing a dissertation can be very lonely for some. Extroverts typically gain energy from being around others and miss those stimulating classroom discussions. The data keep coming as the student begins to feel overwhelmed and just wants to be done. Chairs can help by talking to the student about recognizing that it is a solitary phase and it only lasts a short time. Remind the student that this is an amazing, exciting, and rewarding time for which they've spent years preparing. It is often helpful to students to find another faculty member or committee member with a similar interest or help them connect with someone at another university with whom they can have conversations that keep them excited. They can talk about future research together, help with writing, and in general be a "go to" person.

Missing out on activities with friends and family may seem like a solution to making progress. Sometimes it is important to put away the work and take a break. Students will find that taking a break can freshen their creativity, improve their mood, and in general help them be more productive.

Megan Johnson in her blog on *GradHacker* (2012) addressed the topic of loneliness. Interestingly, she noted that the times when she was most lonely were the times when she was procrastinating or only half-focused on her research. Half-focused means checking Facebook and refreshing your email every 10 seconds. She admits that when she is focused on what she is doing, the work itself keeps her company and time flies by. When we address self-care below, we discuss other indicators to address difficulty concentrating, or as she puts it being half-focused. Most important is helping the student understand the loneliness of extended writing and encouraging self-care.

ENCOURAGING SELF-CARE

Self-care is obviously taking care of yourself and making sure that your health and well-being is a priority in the midst of all of the things going on in life. This goes far beyond brushing your teeth and eating a balanced diet. Self-care is about taking part in activities that are pleasurable, relaxing, and restorative. These activities need be included in the life of graduate students and as Chair, you can encourage students to maintain a healthy balance of research, writing, and personal time.

Students who are working full-time, raising a family, and writing a dissertation are at high risk for burnout. It is easy, over time, to have the overwhelming weight of the dissertation impact every part of the life of the student. They will often say that they will take care of themselves when they finish graduate school. Sometimes, as a Chair, they need to hear our reassurance (and sometimes insistence) to not feel guilty when they are taking a break from their work or are putting the dissertation on the shelf for the weekend in order to spend some time with family.

All graduate students face the pressure to succeed. This might stem from internal or external forces. This pressure can mount and lead to additional challenges to the student, which can lead to some cognitive, emotional, and behavioral roadblocks. What may result is the student stating, "I am not good enough" or "I am not smart enough to do this." Depression is common and may result in the need for medical intervention for the student to move forward.

Having candid conversations about how the student is feeling is especially important during "low" times. As you get to know the student, pay attention to his or her mental health. Consider referring the student to campus resources if you observe trouble brewing or think a student could just use an outlet for stress. Model this as well—talk to the student about how you balanced your busy life during your thesis or dissertation. How did you manage to keep it all together? Sometimes hearing these "war stories" from others can be just the encouragement a student needs.

It is important to note that the prevalence of mental health challenges of doctoral students is higher than the general population. One study reported that one in two doctoral students experiences psychological stress and one in three, a psychiatric illness (Okahana, 2018). It is important to understand the symptoms and signs of depression. Again, be prepared to contact campus mental health resources if you observe that a student may need some outside intervention. One component on which graduate faculty are often undertrained are the symptoms of depression; many graduate deans are left wondering how the faculty can help. As Chair, you are in a prime position to observe and notice if a student needs additional assistance.

> *Case in point: Jackie was finished with her proposal and working toward her defense. She came in for her appointment with Dr. J and it was obvious to Dr. J that she was not doing well. Dr. J observed that she did not make eye contact and was very mechanical in her discussion of her data. When Dr. J made a suggestion about her data the tears began to flow. "I can't do this any longer." Dr. J offered her encouragement and ways to help address the data. But Jackie was just not herself.*
>
> *Dr. J asked if she would like some coffee and left for a minute to get some for both of them. When she came back, Jackie was sobbing. She said, "I might as well tell you, my husband left me for another woman. I don't know if I can make it." After talking more, Jackie told Dr. J that she was having trouble sleeping, was unable to eat, was calling in sick to work at least once a week, and was having no contact with friends and family. Dr. J knew that Jackie was severely depressed and needed help.*
>
> *While Jackie was in the office, Dr. J called the campus counselor and was able to get an immediate appointment. Dr. J walked her across campus to the counseling office. Jackie called Dr. J the next day and set up the next appointment for working on her dissertation and said that she would meet with Dr. J each week right before her counseling session. Jackie graduated and is doing well.*

Graduate students also often view time that they are sleeping as the time they could or should be working on their thesis or dissertation. Findings from the National Collegiate Health Assessment show that 90% of students get five or fewer nights of enough sleep. Even more, 77.1% of students report feeling tired, dragged out, or sleepy two or more days during the week, and 25% experience this five days per week. Sleep deprivation can be a large contributor to difficulty concentrating, which is certainly an unwelcome obstacle to writing. Due to irregular daytime routines, side jobs, and exam periods, students need to be very cognizant to the need for consistent and adequate sleep and sleep patterns (Schlarb, Friedrich, & Claßen, 2017). As Chair, encourage your student to put the work away in order to get adequate rest. Reassure the student that a rested mind is one that can write better and can think more critically.

Exercise is also one overlooked area for many graduate students. Again, it becomes an issue of "I'll do more of it after I graduate." Most of us know the benefits of exercise, but for graduate students who are deeply engaged in high-level cognitive work, exercise is a necessity. Any physical activity will do, whether it is yoga, a quick run, weight lifting, or whatever immediately improves mood and increases the ability to concentrate.

Furthermore, hours sitting in an office chair can lead to blood clots. This, in turns, slows down the body system and causes weight gain, slower processing time, and overall fatigue. Sedentary time needs to balance with active time to increase concentration, limit stress, and strengthen the body's immune system. As Chair, you can model this as well. Share your workout routine with the student. Encourage the student to get up and take walks each hour during writing, to drink some water, and to spend some time moving away from the thesis or dissertation.

Water and Nutrition

Is it our role to talk to the student about water and nutrition? There are times when it is important, and our advice can make a difference in the success of the student. Those conversations are relatively easy and important to model. Even having a bottle of water on our desk is a simple way of showing our commitment to health. Water is known to improve physical performance, help with weight loss, improve mood, increase brain power, prevent headaches, and protect against disease. When you drink more water, your cognitive performance increases. Several studies have found this result in both adults and children. Even mild dehydration can impact cognitive function in the short term (Riebl & Davy, 2013). So remind the students to drink up!

Avoiding the Drive-Thru

Once again, is it our role to talk to students about nutrition and overall wellness? It might be. When our student complains about gaining weight and having trouble maintaining concentration, a short nutrition discussion might help. Avoiding the drive-thru is an easy topic to open this discussion. While it might seem to save time in the short term, in the long term it probably costs more in terms of overall energy and nutrition. Grocery stores and healthier restaurants have delivery services in our larger communities. The Chair could also suggest organizing eating through menu planning. Once again, is it our role to help the student stay healthy? It may be.

> *Case in point: Cindy came in for her appointment with Dr. T with a bag and a drink from a local fast-food restaurant. She groaned, "I feel like all we eat at my house is fast food. I've gained 15 pounds and feel gross." Dr. T spent a few minutes talking to her about the impact of poor nutrition, especially drinking soda rather than water, on overall wellness, improved mood, and cognitive performance. At the next session Cindy came in with a water bottle and an orange and showed her menu for the month. Dr. T laughed and said, "I'm glad you shared that Cindy, but you didn't have to. I knew that you would make changes."*

There is also a critical need for downtime from the high level of engagement required by academic writing. Mindfulness is sometimes defined as a nonjudgmental, present-moment engagement. That is, step away from the writing and engage your mind elsewhere. Mindfulness reduces stress levels, increases calmness, and promotes relaxation. Slowing down the processing of the brain, in turn, slows the churning of the academic mind and unleashes the ability to think and listen to our body. The act of slowing down the thinking process has a side benefit in that once returning to the task at hand, it is with a fresher, clearer thought pattern. Through slowing the mind, we can look at outcomes from multiple vantage points that we had likely not even considered. Optimal performance will result from making mindfulness a habit.

It may take the Chair's guidance to help the students break the work into small tasks. For example, rather than suggesting that the student write the entire literature review, you might suggest that the student work on one specific section of it. Rather than analyzing all findings in one week, encourage the student to break up the task into small segments and utilize a few extra weeks. This segmenting of the tasks may prevent the student from being overwhelmed, and in the long run may promote more student success.

Balancing Relationships

Graduate students in the thesis or dissertation portion of their program must learn to manage life's priorities and demands in order to complete their degree. Some are married, have significant personal relationships, parent children, or have other exceptional life circumstances. Students should be encouraged to find a balance—a course load and writing process that enables them to be present in their life and make progress toward their goal. Some will be unable to do this, while others will do it quite well. It is an individual path and the advice to the graduate student should be to enjoy the challenge of this process, rather than rush through it and miss the intellectual process or slow down and self-destruct along the way. A student with balanced relationships will have an outlet outside of the institution with whom to share insights, challenges, and struggles. The same student, however, will cultivate meaningful relationships with those on campus in order to find a shared commonality in the struggle.

Financial Demands

One aspect of a student's well-being not always noticed or tended to by universities is the financial component of graduate education. Forbes noted that student loan debt is now the second-highest debt category in the United States, topped only by mortgage debt. The average student in the class of 2016 had $37,172 in student loan debt (Friedman, 2018). Some students work multiple jobs to pay for graduate school while others are reliant on student loans or other sources of income to pay for tuition and other living expenses.

When the financial well-being of a student is out of balance, the student may find this to be a source of high stress. While Chairs probably do not delve into the individual finances of students, it is important to realize that some students carry a pressure to complete their degree within a certain time frame in order to control their overall expenses. In addition, others may run out of funding, grants may expire, or money may simply run out.

Chairs should be cognizant that sometimes a student's financial distress may weave its way unknowingly into the thesis or dissertation process and while the Chair has no formal responsibility to help a student manage the overall financial investment, it can be an issue in negotiating time to degree or frustration when an expected graduation date is delayed.

PRACTICE MAKES PERFECT

Scholarly writing is developed over time. Even some of the best academic writers struggle to form sentences, express ideas, and explain concepts. One suggestion we've seen that can be helpful in getting used to the practice of writing can be to find a piece of high-quality, nonfiction writing, and to copy it by hand. Not plagiarize. Just rewrite it, then throw it away. The process of copying someone's writing, in a strange way, helps the student begin to craft higher-quality sentences. Reading informs writing but reading and writing are different neuromotor tasks (Goodson, 2013, p. 71). Copying good form is practicing good writing technique, which in turn can lead to better writing.

Punctuation practice for both fun and learning can be achieved by reading *Eats, Shoots & Leaves* by Lynn Truss (2003). After reading this book, students will find that correcting grammatical errors is easy and can actually be a little bit fun. The idea is that students should not expect perfection in their first encounter with a paper. In fact, they should expect to make many, many mistakes, to rewrite many pages, and to throw some of their work away. Encourage students to become comfortable not only as scholars, but also as writers. Help students to see themselves develop as writers.

Resources to Share with Students

While many thesis and dissertation textbooks provide guidance on the "how" and "why" of writing the formal paper, there are a few resources that provide some guidance on how to handle the challenge of graduate school and how to navigate the pressures within. A few we recommend are as follows:

- *The Portable Dissertation Advisor* by Miles Bryant. Chapter 7 in particular offers sound advice on health issues, quitting, and issues with completion.
- *The Dissertation Journey: A Practical and Comprehensive Guide to Planning, Writing, and Defending Your Dissertation* by Carol Roberts. This book describes the dissertation process as a "journey" and helps students navigate the ups and downs of its travels.
- *Surviving Your Thesis* by Suzan Burton and Peter Steane offers a sound level of supportive advice that begins with the reader asking about the thesis process, "Is this right for me?"

POINTS TO CONSIDER

- Understand that some students do not complete the process. It happens. Be OK with this. Realize that it is not a reflection of your work or effort.
- Be aware of a student's mental health. If you see warning signs of depression or anxiety, be ready to refer the student to campus or community mental health resources.
- Learn about appropriate campus and community mental health resources. Have pamphlets or contact information readily available for when you need to share it with a student.
- Talk to students about taking care of themselves physically with regular exercise, adequate water, and good food choices. Help them understand how their choices in these areas impact their ability to think, write, and maintain extended concentration.
- Encourage students. This sounds simple but sometimes we end up as critics more than mentors. Find a balance between critical feedback and

positive reinforcement. Authentic feedback will always build a stronger scholar.

- Suggest that the student find an emotional support group of fellow students or others navigating the writing process. Sometimes having a community of others can provide positive feedback and emotional support needed by a graduate student.
- Encourage the student to step away for the weekend to come back strong. Put the writing away and enjoy some time with family and friends.

Chapter Seven

Common Writing Issues

CASE STUDY—PART 7

Student was making progress on his dissertation and was sharing drafts with Chair every few weeks. Student had been a strong writer in his graduate coursework and knew how to approach writing a term paper with ease. His citations weren't always perfect, but he managed to muddle through with good grades. When he received his latest draft back from Chair, he was mortified at the comments she provided.

She highlighted areas that were not cited properly and mentioned that they could be considered plagiarism. She offered revisions for sentences and drew arrows to move entire sections of papers from one chapter of the paper to another. This perplexed Student. He was now familiar with the setup but was unsure of what went where and how his work suddenly seemed so inadequate. He took a deep breath and dove into his revisions but was lost. Should he seek out an editor? Did someone else need to read his work? Was he just not good enough to be an academic writer?

- *What writing issues should a Chair prioritize when helping emerging scholars?*
- *What tools can the Chair provide to assist with organization and overall layout of the thesis or dissertation?*
- *What considerations should Chair make when providing feedback?*

A blank page can be ominous and miserable to the author confronting it. It is difficult for us, as seasoned scholars who have earned degrees through a thesis or dissertation, to get started, so how can we help our students begin writing their own theses or dissertations? One piece of advice we have heard over the years is that the student (the writer) needs to bleed on the page. Just write. Hemingway suggested this and went back and said he might keep one sentence of his "shitty" first draft. As writers, we often feel inadequate or simply unable to write for academic settings. How can we help students move beyond the ominous feeling they get when looking at a blank page with sometimes hundreds more remaining to write?

GUIDING STUDENT WRITING

Just Write

For the student who is a perfectionist, he or she may want to develop an outline. Many authors are adamantly opposed to this because it will eventually lead to a writer's block. Using a mind map might be a better choice because new branches can be linked. A mind map is a diagram for representing tasks, words, concepts, or items linked to and arranged around a central concept or subject using a nonlinear graphical layout that allows the user to build an intuitive framework around a central concept. A mind map can turn a long list of monotonous information into a colorful, memorable, and highly organized diagram that works in line with the brain's natural way of doing things. Having a mind map puts ink to paper, and the next step is helping students become motivated to sit down and write. There are many ways to do this—with pen and paper, with colored highlighters, using a computer app, or using a commercial organizational software.

Bring Out the Mind Map

Now sit down and put those branches into sentences and paragraphs. But, in come the excuses. "I can't find the time to write, which unfortunately means I find other tasks that are either more interesting or easier to accomplish." There are a couple of ways to help students overcome the avoidance of sitting down to write.

One is keeping a journal that includes the starting time, the ending time, what they accomplished, and where they need to begin the next writing session. Students create competitions with themselves to increase their writing time, and it helps them get started with the next writing session. In addition, encouraging students to find a community of writers, maybe even fellow graduate students, might be motivational and help the student stay focused on the task ahead. When students know where to start their next writing session and that others are doing the same arduous tasks, it is far easier for them to write on a regular basis.

ORGANIZATION

Most graduate students are equipped with a natural motivation and upon generating a mind map or other organizational planning piece, can start to "bleed" those ideas on paper. The initial production of writing is scattered, messy, and often incomplete. Encourage the student to write focused on ideas, rather than grammar and spelling. As writing begins to take shape, students can then polish, prune, sharpen, and double check the text they are generating. Revising is an important step that students fail to realize is so critical to academic writing, but it is also something that should not be heavily enforced in the beginning stages of drafting. While careful writing should be encouraged, often students need to play with words and get ideas on paper before the actual academic pieces and the professional writing can then be formed.

Editing and proofreading are vastly different. Students need to understand that both are necessary. Editing involves organizing ideas, connecting sentences, and moving paragraphs. Reverse outlining helps to make sure structures are in place and the text flows (Goodson, 2013). Accomplishing this requires the writer to read the complete text, move the paragraphs, then sentences, and finally simple phrases. By reading the text from big ideas to small phrases, the writer can begin to see how the words fit together and flow of writing begins. Editing is only part of the task, however.

Proofreading, in contrast to editing, involves checking for errors, correcting inconsistencies that include format, grammar, punctuation, and spelling. Proofreading can be difficult for students who do not have a strong background in it, so the use of a professional editor or campus writing service may be necessary. Discuss this with your student to determine his or her strengths with proofreading. It is important to be honest about one's ability in order to save time during the drafting process. Some students expect Chairs to edit their work. While this may be your preference, it can also be an arduous process and one that we question may not be appropriate for a graduate-level student.

THE CONCRETE PLAN

Providing students with a step-by-step list or checklist to the overall thesis or dissertation process can help a student stay focused and anticipate the next step in the process. It can also be used to show students how much they have accomplished and what lies ahead. Explaining the steps can be relatively simple and advising with a step by step plan like this one:

Step 1: Engaging in a conceptual conversation
Step 2: Creating the dissertation preproposal

Step 3: Approval of a preproposal or idea paper by your advisor
Step 4: Collecting the literature
Step 5: Coding the literature
Step 6: Writing the literature
Step 7: Writing the proposal
Step 8: Review of the proposal by your advisor
Step 9: Revising the proposal
Step 10: Defending the proposal
Step 11: Obtaining human subjects' approval
Step 12: Collecting the data
Step 13: Transforming the data to codable form
Step 14: Coding the data
Step 15: Developing a schema to explain the data
Step 16: Writing a sample analysis
Step 17: Review of the sample analysis
Step 18: Writing the findings or chapter or chapters
Step 19: Writing the final chapter
Step 20: Transforming the proposal into a chapter or chapters and preparing the front matter
Step 21: Editing the chapters
Step 22: Review by your advisor
Step 23: Revising
Step 24: Approval by the graduate school
Step 25: Making final formatting revisions
Step 26: Review by your committee members
Step 27: Defending
Step 28: Revising
Step 29: Submitting (Foss and Waters, 2007, pp.18–22)

THE PREPROPOSAL (OR PROSPECTUS)

It is also helpful for students to put together a preproposal, or prospectus, to help lay out the major pieces of the proposed thesis or dissertation (Foss & Waters, 2007). This type of preplanning encourages critical thinking at an early stage and forces the student to begin to conceptualize the reality of the study they propose to complete. At the completion of a preproposal, the Chair is able to help the student further develop and realign the study as needed. If nothing else, it forces the student to put work on paper and to begin to see how the puzzle pieces of the thesis or dissertation will fit together.

Following is an example a preproposal template; consider giving your students some sort of organizer listing the required components of your institution's thesis or dissertation format. The more tools you can provide the student, the more organized the researcher can then be. An outline for pre-proposal can be crafted to meet the committee's and Chair's requirements, and could look something like this:

1. Introduction to the problem

    a. Why is this issue important? What problem are you trying to address?
    b. One to two pages with appropriate citations.

2. Operational Definitions

    a. Define only the major concepts, programs, and variables.
    b. Define all key terms as you use them for reader comprehension throughout the preproposal.

3. Framework

    a. What is the theoretical, conceptual, or perceptual frame foundational to this study?
    b. Less than one page with appropriate citations.

4. Reasons that the study is significant

    a. What are the broad, deep implications for educational and academic merit? What are the implications for educational leadership (or other area of study)?
    b. Approximately one to two pages with citations.

5. Purpose statement

    a. One specific sentence.
    b. "Therefore the purpose of this _____ study will be to (explore/discover/describe) (the central phenomenon) for (participants) (when and where)."

6. Central Research Question

    a. Begin with how or what (not why)—open ended.
    b. Specify the central phenomenon and variables with neutral language.

    c. Remember that this is the overarching or general question that delineates what is in and out of the scope of the research. (Help the student make the wording of their question clear!)

    d. It is optional to add sub-questions if they help explain the variables or factors involved. These are more specific and can help organize the study.

    e. Remind the student that the research questions are not the questions asked of participants!

7. Profile of data collection and analysis—questions for students

    a. Research Design—What is the method proposed, and why is it appropriate?

    b. Data—What is the source of data, and how do we have ethical access to it?

    c. Collection—What are your procedures or steps to gather information?

    d. Analysis—What form will your analysis take? How will the findings be reported?

    e. Strength of Claims Made—How will you show the power of your research in your study?

8. Plan for the Review of Literature Section

    a. What are the outline, literature map, or major categories that will be covered in the proposal to support the understanding of the study? (Further literature will be gathered after the data is collected and cannot be outlined at this point—so is not part of the preproposal.)

    b. Graphic is possible, but detail and organization in narrative form is required, two pages maximum.

9. Organization of the Study and Future Steps

    a. How will the student present the study in logical order? What does the student still need to think about and get clarification about to answer their research question?

    b. Less than one page, but more informational than a list of chapters.

10. References in correct APA format (based upon Foss & Waters, 2007)

The results of this are very preliminary. After all, this is a drafting tool, but it does allow the Chair and committee to determine whether the student has the background knowledge required to complete the thesis or dissertation.

BUILDING HABITS WITH ONLINE TOOLS

In addition to helping students understand scholarly writing, it may be necessary to take the time to help the student develop a writing system. For example, when the student includes a citation, encourage the student to stop and write the citation in the reference section in order to save going back and digging through a pile of articles to find the reference information later. One of the first writing challenges we can address is organization—that is, organization of the writer as opposed to the writing product itself. Students are typically not familiar with the piles of research articles, books, and "stuff" that come along with writing this major paper and if we can help address this as Chair, we can help remove some of the ambiguity of "What do I do next?" or "How can I get this accomplished?"

Students who have difficulty organizing their lives may save work in multiple places and forget where it was saved. We've seen this on multiple flash drives, drafts saved under numerical titles that can never be remembered, and drives cluttered with unfinished chapters. Students should be encouraged to use cloud storage like Box, DropBox, Google Drive, Amazon Drive, and OneDrive. This not only allows access at multiple locations but ensures that the work will not be deleted or destroyed should a laptop be stolen or a computer destroyed.

Additionally, there are some free, open-source cloud platforms that work very well for this purpose. A few examples include OwnCloud, NextCloud, Seafile, Pydio, Tonido, Cozy, and Syncthing (Mauya, 2018). Saving the drafts in multiple places, while important to prevent loss of work, can also lead to much confusion if there is not some semblance of order to the work. Encourage students to formulate an organization and naming structure that clearly identifies the part of the writing being stored as well as the last date worked on the draft.

Programs that help students prepare reference or bibliography information may be advantageous for some students. Some we have seen students use with some ease include Noodletools or RefWorks. These tools have been around for several decades, are inexpensive, and cycle through continuous improvement based upon updates so that the programs integrate easily with other software that has also had major updates. Other citation software includes Zotero, Citation Machine, Easy Bib, Bib Me, and CloudCite. These programs are online and usually store references in a specific format you select. If you need to find the name of a book that you used three years ago, you will find it in your reference files.

Besides storing references, most of these programs have additional organization tools that students can use to support and organize their work. Most importantly, helping students develop a system that works for them is the key. For example, help them create a routine for saving references as they write. As a note of caution, students still need to learn their fundamental citation formatting. That is, while these electronic programs assist with ease of use and storing resources, they are also not 100% perfect.

Grammarly is an online grammar checking, spell checking, and plagiarism detection program. In addition to simple grammar checking, it reminds you of passive voice, wordiness, overused words, miswritten words, contextual spelling, and vocabulary enhancement. The program makes it easy to revise as you write. While grammar is not always the focus of one's writing at times, it is important that students effectively manage their grammar and spelling in order to prepare professional communication and academic writing. This program has a small fee associated with it, yet is highly recommended for thesis and dissertation writers who become immune to seeing errors on their pages.

TIGHTEN IT UP

Teaching a student to create a tight, or concise, paragraph requires teaching consistency and the purpose of the paragraph itself. First, the paragraph should open with a strong lead-in or topic sentence. Second, the transition should follow a topic or key sentence. Third, the rest of the paragraph should provide support or evidence for the idea in the key sentence (Gray, 2005). An easy way to teach this is to have the student highlight the main idea sentence and to make sure that there is a connection to the previous paragraph. Working with these key sentences is an important step to creating flow in writing. The key sentence work will also help the students dump or move topics that are out of context. Typically, students try to write like scholars—that is, in a voice or tone that is not personal. While professional writing is critical, so, too, is a student's unique style and voice. When students pretend to write like professors, they can usually only do so for a short time before running to a thesaurus or spinning ideas into a web of incoherency.

EMPTYING THE TRASH

Cleaning up a cluttered paper involves line by line revising. Have the student read the text out loud to themselves to determine if it sounds as it was intended is a great strategy to help identify poor writing or grammatical errors. Two books often recommended to graduate students are Strunk and White's *The Element of Style* and *Stylish Academic Writing* by Helen Sword. It is important for students to realize that not every word they write will end up in the final thesis or dissertation.

Writing is a process—and sometimes that process ends up with work in the trash bin. Letting go of carefully written sections can be difficult, but encourage students to find peace in the process of simplifying and clarifying their work. All good writers put work in the trash, so writing a thesis or dissertation should be no different. Encourage students to do this. It does not devalue the investment in the writing, but rather allows the strongest pieces to remain part of the living document. In addition, it is much easier to remove work than it is to add pages and pages from nothing. Deleting and removing words and pages is a much easier task than building from the ground up.

USING PROFESSIONAL VOICE

A professional writing voice comes with practice. One way to increase vocabulary is to read—a lot. Helping students with academic writing means helping them recognize high-quality academic writing in their field, which in turn means that the more they read, the closer to academic writing their own work will become. When students study other writers, they begin to see nuances in an author's writing.

In addition, they will begin to see the necessity of clarity and professionalism. Rarely will they find jargon or casual phrasing. Author Helen Sword writes about putting your writing on a diet—that is, finding ways to eliminate jargon and unnecessary sentences. Writing should be very clear and concise. Ernest Hemingway once said, "My aim is to put down on paper what I see and what I feel in my best and simplest way" (Hemingway, n.d.). Each student has a writer's voice and our role as Chair is to help them put it on paper and be proud of it.

PLAGIARISM

Plagiarism should be discussed with every thesis or dissertation student with whom you work. In essence, students need to know that we should never claim the words and ideas of others as our own and should give credit where credit is due. Students may not purposefully engage in plagiarism and may need to be reminded of APA Ethics Code Standard 8.1.1:

As stated in the sixth edition of the *Publication Manual of the American Psychological Association* (APA, 2010), the ethical principles of scientific publication are designed to ensure the integrity of scientific knowledge and to protect the intellectual property rights of others. As the *Publication Manu-*

al explains, authors are expected to correct the record if they discover errors in their publications; they are also expected to give credit to others for their prior work when it is quoted or paraphrased.

Regardless of whether you are utilizing the APA as your citation style, plagiarism is generally considered an academic misconduct offense and may be subject to penalties within an institution. If a student is caught purposefully plagiarizing work, nearly all graduate schools will have guidelines to follow for disciplinary measures.

In order to avoid plagiarism, graduate students often overcite the works of others or use long, direct passages in a block quotation. In general, the APA *Publication Manual* recommends one to two direct quotations for each topic in a paper. That is, direct quotations should be minimal and only used when necessary. Part of the hurdle with citations is helping the student understand that his or her own academic voice is most important and the quotes from other authors support the student voice. Encourage students to manage their citations as they write. There are numerous online programs that will help the student format and save citations, and their sanity when they finish the paper.

It is important, as the Chair, that you know what to do when you face an instance of plagiarism. That is, what are the institutional rules and procedures? What needs to be reported and what simply needs to be rewritten? And how will you approach a student you believe has plagiarized work? What if the student denies the accusation? Or becomes angry or aggressive? Most students struggle with the balance of citing sources and overciting sources, and sometimes this takes a bit of conversation to find the right balance; however, it can become a grave ethical challenge when you learn that a scholar is presenting someone else's work as his or her own. Understand that these situations typically require institutional notice and seek guidance from your contacts within the department as to how best to navigate a plagiarism situation.

THE INTERNET AND OTHER WRITING TEMPTATIONS

Something to note of more recent development is the entry of the internet (and its multitude of sites and information) that can assist (and deter) a graduate student during the writing process. While there are some great sites to help students with writing techniques, citation and reference development, and scholarly research, so too is there a myriad of distractions and ethical danger zones of which students should be wary.

Today there are sites where a student can pay a fee to have a thesis or dissertation written by an anonymous writer online (sometimes for several thousand dollars). There are other sites where data can be quickly developed by an unknown source. And there are yet other sites offering individualized thesis and dissertation coaching and academic guidance. While such sites might be scams or ways for ghost writers to earn some easy money, graduate students need to be aware of the dangers of hiring someone to write their paper or securing some other source to gather data. The integrity of a student under stress can sometimes be tested and the internet provides some easy ways to seek out shortcuts to the hard work required to complete a thesis or dissertation. Rather than ignore that these services exist, talk with the student about how such services can raise ethical flags and credibility questions about the student's work.

SYNTHESIS

A thesis or dissertation requires the student's ability to synthesize multiple sources of research to justify the study proposed. This is sometimes the most difficult skill to teach students because it requires abstract thought and conceptualization of more than one idea. The literature review is an integral part of the thesis or dissertation that encompasses what the academic world has already published about the topic and provides a basis of learning and content on which the graduate student can build an original study.

This is often the most arduous task for the thesis or dissertation student—that is, the literature review can be a complex chapter to write and students often face writing issues when trying to synthesize multiple sources. It could be helpful to assist students in learning when and where they synthesize information—and to realize that they do this quite often when writing papers for coursework or publication. Carol Roberts (2010) presents a list of when students synthesize information. This list includes when students:

- identify relationships among studies;
- compare and contrast the ideas, theories, and concepts of multiple authors;
- comment on common themes emerging from the readings;
- discuss the pros and cons;
- explain a conflict or contradiction among sources;
- point out gaps in the literature;
- identify inconsistencies and make generalizations about studies;
- make connections between sources; and
- discuss how literature informs the topic being studied. (pp. 100–101)

As this list demonstrates, the literature review need not be an abstract form. Students have practiced these skills and are able to read multiple sources in an analytical fashion. For the thesis or dissertation, they just need to begin thinking more widely about what they've read and how the readings interact. The student must be able to draw together those sources and respond with their own ideas. A literature review should not be a retelling of study findings or participant groups, but rather a carefully articulated discussion of the larger discipline as a field of study.

REVISION

The first draft is complete—finally. The student is excited at the sense of accomplishment. He or she may also be exhausted. It is a good time to encourage taking a few days or even a week to relax and let it go, to reenergize for that last lap.

Revision can actually be fun. Rereading the draft leads students to think about what they have said, polish, think of new ideas to add, and revise, revise, revise. The students will read the sentences they wrote and discover clearer ways to say the same things. It can be helpful to students to think about reading this from the point of view of another person such as their mom or a friend from another country. Is it understandable? Feedback from others can be confusing. As stated earlier, creating a color-coded system separating feedback into must change, might change, and do not change (just a thought to share) helps the student decide what is required, what to think about, and what must be deleted.

Alison Miller (2009) shares her three concrete strategies in her book *Finish your Dissertation Once and For All!* that can be employed to help students understand the process of revision. First, encourage the student to print out a single-sided copy of the entire paper with pagination. Students may be accustomed to scrolling up and down on the page to make revisions. Revising individual sentences and paragraphs is easy to do directly on a screen. Reorganization of a chapter or substantial revisions is much easier to manage with a print copy. Laying the papers side by side and seeing larger parts can help students see the thesis or dissertation as a whole and help them revise the organization of the paper and look for repetition, misused words, and other errors.

Second, if the revisions are substantial, or based upon feedback from one or more other people, it is a good idea to make an inventory or itemized list of the changes you will need to make prior to revising. There will be line-by-line edits and then substantial edits. Next, the student should read through the entire document with a judicious eye to find other errors. Next, if there are questions for the reviewer, it is a good time to note the change that the student questions. Next, encourage the student to read through the document and make an inventory list based upon their own instincts.

The third strategy is to have the student read his or her work and deconstruct it in some way. This deconstruction process means that the student will read the draft to determine what has been written, what seems out of place, what seems missing, what is worth keeping, and what needs substantial revision or reorganization. This might include a reverse outline of what has already been written. This might simply mean a list of headings, points made under each heading, and notes about what is confusing or disorganized. The deconstruction list can involve making notes to oneself about additional material that needs to be added along with questions and dilemmas to discuss with someone. Finally, reading the paper aloud will help the student uncover additional errors or missing pieces that need to be included, and will give an assurance that the document flows (Miller, 2009).

STEPPING AWAY FROM THE PAPER

When one gets embroiled in the writing process, it can be difficult to see gaps, holes, and errors. That is, the author can become almost too familiar with the writing and can fail to see where an outside reader might be confused or need further clarification. It is a wise idea to advise students to step away from their work—take a meaningful break, sleep on it, and pick it up with fresh eyes another day. Granted, this will take time; setting the paper down and allowing the passage of time to create distance does in fact require time, but the time away is extremely valuable in the writing process.

One can begin to reflect on writing and on the goals and aims of the paper, and perhaps even begin to identify new ideas and directions. This is a difficult thing to encourage students to do—many want to send a draft to Chair review only to continue to constantly rewrite and revise while the Chair is finding time to provide feedback. Ask students to take a purposeful writing break and to take time to renew their minds before reengaging with their work. It seems a bit counterintuitive to let time pass, but the rejuvenation that comes from a mental break can be priceless.

POINTS TO CONSIDER

- Help students face that blank page with a *mind map* and a writing journal that keeps track of the time that they have spent writing and the topic they need to face when starting the next writing session. The journal will be a source of motivation and help them stay organized.
- Guide the student into creating clear and concise work. Hemingway described his writing thusly: "My aim is to put down on paper what I see and what I feel in my best and simplest way."
- Encourage the student to develop a writing voice and be proud of it.
- A Chinese proverb advises, "You give a poor man a fish, and you feed him for a day. You teach him to fish, and you give him an occupation that will feed him for a lifetime." Keep in mind that serving as a Chair for a

thesis or dissertation is teaching. In our service to the students, we are lifting them to a new level of academic rigor.

Chapter Eight

Problems, Delays, and Misunderstandings— Motivation and Insight

CASE STUDY—PART 8

Chair noticed that each meeting with Student was becoming frostier, with defensive replies and almost hostile looks becoming more prevalent. There was nothing new that Chair was aware of except that Student had planned to graduate this year and the slow progress made that goal unlikely.

- *How deeply should Chair dig into what could be a personal problem of Student's? Is there any harm in letting things develop naturally?*
- *What can Chair do to open a conversation on the slow progress?*
- *If trust has been broken, how can the relationship be mended?*

As the Chair and candidate work independently and together to complete the study, it is normal for problems, delays, and misunderstandings to arise. A thesis or dissertation is novice research, so candidates may have unrealistic expectations of the effort involved or underestimate the need to work within the university, department, and Chair's oversight. Many times, redefining the purpose, clarifying expectations, and setting up goals and benchmarks are all that is needed to get back on track in troublesome spots. While the first step in working with students is to listen carefully before advising, a close second is to reassure them that the difficulties, motivation lags, and frustrations are normal. A butterfly must struggle out of the cocoon to have the strength to fly, and those completing a thesis or dissertation must grapple with the content, methods, and significance of the work to have the power to defend and publish it.

New Chairs soon learn that their role is not only to outline and support the work to be done, but also to build the relationship. So, while the initial conversations have a focus on what the dissertation topic will be, how deep and broad is the significance, how available are the data and participants, and so on, the Chair's target is gaining familiarity with the candidate. It is relatively easy to create a blueprint for successful research in the abstract—the candidates bring the complexity not only in how they approach the research, but ultimately in how they cope with life under stress.

In the marathon task of a completing a thesis or dissertation, all students "hit the wall." Expecting setbacks is a good conversation to have early in the process and should be repeated often. No study is perfect, all research has flaws, research-based writing is unique and taxing, data is not always available as planned, meeting all committee members' expectations is tricky— there are tough times in every study.

Unfortunately, Chairs soon learn that the normal candidate responses are panic, getting advice from friends instead of experts, anger and blaming others, and self-doubt and despair. Responding to the rough patches without being defensive or taking responsibility is the art of Chairing dissertations and theses, and no two candidates respond in the same manner. But the common way to address small and large problems is to have laid down the framework in advance by building a good professional relationship. Candidates do not need a Chair's sympathy; they need empathy. Sympathy is sharing the experience, and they have other people in their lives with whom to commiserate. Empathy is understanding the experience and maintaining enough distance from the problem to be able to see it from many perspectives and separate emotions from options.

Yet while each candidate is unique, there are patterns of issues that arise during the process and categories of typical responses. Part of building the relationship is looking for the way candidates view themselves, respond when stressed, and motivate themselves. A Chair who reads the style of their candidate accurately may minimize and hopefully prevent common dissertation or thesis problems.

BUILDING RELATIONSHIP THROUGH UNDERSTANDING STYLE

To explain human behavior, Brinkman and Kirschner (2012) developed a lens of understanding by determining how *assertive* a person is in a situation (from passive to aggressive) and where they place their *focus* (task or people). By intersecting these two continuums, four zones of behavior appear.

Everyone is motivated by one or more of these zones at any given time, but the inner and outer environment move emphasis from one intent to another. The four intents are:

1. Get It Done (assertive task focus),
2. Get It Right (passive task focus),
3. Get Along (passive people focus), and
4. Get Appreciated (assertive task focus; Brinkman & Kirschner, 2012).

Graduate students under the pressure of research development feel all of these intents, and a Chair who frames the feedback, suggestions, and praise to satisfy these intents has a higher likelihood of being not only heard but useful to the candidate.

Beginning the Process With Get It Done Intent

Framing a study concept is often impacted by the predominant style of the candidate. Those who prefer to view progress through the lens of Get It Done have strengths in setting deadlines, getting to the point in meetings and in writing, and beginning with a targeted goal in mind.

It becomes the Chair's role to broaden and deepen the significance of research, to prepare the candidate for the inevitable setbacks in the complexity of the planning, and to set the relationship so that dialog and revision are not viewed as prevaricating and criticism, but instead as the most effective way of reaching mutual goals. Dealing with ambiguities and delays are frustrating to Get It Done candidates, and getting concise, concrete directions is appreciated.

Beginning the Process With Get It Right Intent

Get It Right candidates think ahead to avoid needless mistakes and pay close attention to details in directions and editing. When initially framing the research, they may refrain from discussing their topic until they have all the components set to their own standards. They may work more slowly than those whose priority is to Get It Done, but deliberation and looking carefully at all aspects is also a strength in thesis and dissertation writing.

This candidate may leave questions unasked rather than appear ignorant to the Chair, so trust building is essential. Praising when the candidate is attempting reasonable risks and setting down motivating benchmarks for progress may become the Chair's role with a Get It Right candidate.

Beginning the Process With Get Along Intent

Working on a dissertation or thesis with a Get Along candidate is rewarding because the priority is to please the Chair, and it is pleasant to interact with people who value positive relationships. However, the process may seem successful to the Chair at times when the candidate is actually frustrated. It is more important to this candidate not to make waves than to voice an opinion or raise a question that could lead to conflict. Therefore, for these students, framing the study is an exercise in finding out the Chair's preferences and pet peeves, and working to meet those guides.

The Chair's role is to dig deep to understand the needs of a Get Along candidate; sometimes the student says he or she understands or does not have questions to please the committee members, and then is stuck or lost. In times of stress, a Get Along can even express a "whatever you want" façade to the point that they are not utilizing their expertise or passion. Regular reassurance, and praising independent initiative, can aid the Chair in motivating the Get Along writer.

Beginning the Process With Get Appreciation Intent

Getting Appreciation from people is an intent that serves the candidate well in crafting a study that will be significant so that others care about the content and generalizable so that others may use the format, framework, and results. The Chair can frame suggestions for change as ways to get people to learn from the research because this candidate is attracted to making a difference.

Seeking appreciation is such a powerful motivating force that the initial idea for research is often too deep and broad for the candidate to graduate in a timely manner. Finding the significance in a narrowed topic may not seem prestigious enough to be appreciated, so it can help in that instance to create hypothetical, narrowed topics and share audiences and publications that would value the work. Then the discussion moves toward several options for narrowing the topic that the candidate can use to match his or her interest.

THREATENED INTENT AND EMERGING CONFLICTS

When fear overshadows normal behavior, a person moves from intent to *threatened intent* (Brinkman & Kirschner, 2012). As the normal intent is not being met, a person moves to behavior that is more extreme, and more difficult to address as a Chair. The intents morph in predictable intensities:

- Get It Done becomes Controlling
- Get It Right becomes Perfectionist
- Get Along becomes Approval Seeking

- Get Appreciated becomes Attention Getting

When these negative behaviors appear, especially early in the writing progression, the Chair may be able to prevent greater conflict by emphasizing the positive intent. For example, if a candidate seems bossy, pushy, or aggressive, and the controlling behavior is setting up a power struggle, it is possible to reframe these actions as wanting to Get It Done—a positive intent. (It never hurts to attribute positive intent to people; sometimes they adopt the positive, and even if they do not, positive thinking keeps one from dwelling on the negative.)

So if that pushy candidate sends an all-caps email stating the Chair's edits are unnecessary and it is time to move to defense, rather than responding to the anger the Chair's reply could be, "I appreciate your goal of working efficiently. Addressing the suggested edits now may allow you to be effective in successfully defending your work with fewer required rewrites." Short and to the point, because those who Get It Done do not admire long explanations. By acknowledging that getting done is also the Chair's intent, and that this intent may be best fulfilled through editing now rather than in the more fearful defense setting, compliance is more likely. A candidate working from this controlling intent will not send an apology for the flaming email because there is a blindness to confrontational tone—but the intent of the Chair is not approval seeking either.

Graduate students have had many years to practice student-teacher relationships, and they have spent countless hours learning to read teachers' nonverbal or implied messages and idiosyncrasies. They bring this ability to the Chair-candidate relationship. In most cases, it smooths the formulation of a team to create a successful thesis or dissertation. Chairs have varying degrees of experience in teaching and working with graduate students, so they often fall back on their own experience to reflect upon the work. If balanced with listening to the candidate and teaming with other professors when issues arise, this combination of memories and trialing is sufficient to build the study and the relationship. However, when the candidate has felt successful over time in utilizing their preferred zone of threatened intent (controlling or perfectionist, approval or attention seeking) and approach the situation with that lens, conflict often manifests. Organizing these conflicts by zone may also suggest ways of addressing solutions.

Get It Done

Those stuck in the controlling aspect of Get It Done zone see themselves as direct, bottom-line, outgoing, and efficient. They may put up a full-frontal attack, or subtly wait for a perceived weakness and pounce. Long discussions, brainstorming, experimenting with several alternatives, and reflecting are considered wasting valuable time. They do not appreciate the advice to explore wider or deeper avenues, to talk with other experts with different views, or to enjoy the journey of graduate work. Their Chairs may be confronted with one of the following situations when trying to develop the frame of the research.

Deadline Driven

If the conversation opens with the plan to get to graduation by a certain date, a deadline driven candidate is almost a certainty. It does not work to redirect the question, "How soon do I graduate?" with "How fast can you write?" What is really being communicated is that a time table is needed, and if not offered will remain a distraction in the rest of the conversation. Chairs sometimes forget that for students this is novice research, and the rhythms and habits Chairs have developed as researchers and writers are unknown to the candidate.

Deadline driven candidates are confident in their writing and research topic. They see the process as trying to beat classmates to defense and the Chair and committee as dragging their feet. Their meetings begin with, "So how soon do I have to defend to graduate this May?" even if the writing is nowhere in sight or near completion. They feel better when controlling the conversation and the Chair, but have less tolerance of the steps and the procedures needed to complete the project.

Changing the subject away from the graduation time line would seem like more foot dragging, so the Chair should simply give the information. When told how many weeks the Chair needs to read a draft, how early in a semester a finished draft must be published to meet university deadlines, and times a candidate must allow the committee to read and give feedback, it becomes apparent to the candidate that this is a different process than writing a paper for class, and sometimes that a dissertation is more prolonged than a thesis. Setting benchmarks helps this candidate but writing them down—including the knowledge that an extension or delay sets back all future benchmarks—keeps the Chair from discovering that the candidate only heard the graduation date and has applied for graduation without completing the thesis or dissertation.

Prepackaged Data

Extreme Get It Done candidates look first for the most direct route to graduation, sacrificing quality, learning, and sometimes even common sense. They look about them for data that is convenient and seems easy to analyze, whether or not it is a well-planned or needed study. It is the Chair's responsibility to point out that low-hanging fruit is not the most desirable if it is mushy or rotten at the core.

> *Case in point: When Dr. Z had his initial meeting with Tess, he knew from teaching her in class that she liked to get to the point quickly. He started the conversation by asking what topics she was considering, and Tess answered that she already knew what she was going to do. She had the database of information from the school district where she worked, and she was going to do a regression on factors impacting teacher satisfaction. She pulled out pie charts and tables she had done in statistics class on the data and was ready to get down to details. It shocked her to be told that she did not have ethical access to use the data, the background knowledge necessary to support the research, or a sufficient avenue of new research to explore.*

Candidates like Tess are easy to move through the process once it is agreed upon. The Chair has no worries that the work will be done, or that she will procrastinate. But the Chair's hardest conversation is to say no to an idea. The candidate is so sure that the idea is relevant and exciting (meaning quick and practical) and the temptation is to let it go forward so the candidate learns from the experience the hard way. This candidate will not learn, but will continue to beat the dead horse, so it is much kinder and more efficient to eliminate the prepackaged idea from the beginning. Even if the idea comes from another faculty member or peer, unless the candidate has the skills and the attitude to truly engage in the research, frustration will arise from thin input and superficial findings. No matter what topic is finally determined, there will be a need to continue coaching to make the effort to have quality, detailed work. If the candidate quotes, "A good dissertation is a done dissertation," the reply is, "An accepted dissertation is a thorough dissertation!"

Better Mousetrap

Sometimes it is the conclusion rather than the data that the candidate has predetermined. When he or she wants to prove something, this preconceived agenda biases the ability to create research than can stand up to defense.

> *Case in point: Dr. H soon became aware that Marc loved the topic of personal online use in a workplace. He became very animated when talking about the topic, but soon gravitated toward the approach that he and his company developed. Marc was disappointed when Dr. H kept moving the topic to a broader scope and tried harder to get her to see that he wanted to evaluate his company's solution so that other companies could use it as a model. Dr. H became more exasperated with his inability or unwillingness to explore a true research question with unknown results and finally told Marc that he was too invested in the topic to have an objective view. Marc requested a change of Chair and thought Dr. H had poisoned the other possible Chairs' opinions when they had the same misgivings. Rather than change topics, Marc is still ABD and trying to market his online watchdog program.*

Candidates like Marc who have the answer before asking the question are often the ones who enter the graduate program knowing their thesis or dissertation topic. Early discussion about the evils of being committed too soon in the research, too biased to be objective, or too dependent upon one answer is vital. A good avenue for a Chair is to start the candidate on seeking an area of expertise rather than a topic at first. Asking "How do you want to be known as the regional or national expert?" "If you were sent to the library to get five books to read this month, what would they be about?" and "Imagine yourself giving the speech of your lifetime, and share what you would want your listeners to remember" can get to those bigger aspirations. That is the field of expertise that the student has enough passion for to persist through tough times. The candidate's research is a thin slice of that bigger expertise.

Get It Right

When perfectionism becomes an issue, the candidate sees this as a strength of being precise, well-written, and deeply grounded as an expert. This is true. It is also an excuse for not moving forward. Or not being wrong. Or not committing to a topic. When a candidate shields vulnerability in perfectionism, they find ways to "spin their wheels" or look like there is progress when there is stalled frustration or action that is not productive. This appears in the process in several different ways.

Still Reading

These candidates often bring piles of books, binders of articles, or stacks of paper to meetings. They are not ready to write because they say they do not know enough and have a lot of sources left to read. As they read, they discover more authors and topics they need to read before they can write. Paul Silvia, author of *How to Write a Lot* (2007), calls this the most insidious of all barriers to writing. There are always more articles to read, more areas to research, and more ways to pretend that taking notes is writing. These candidates spend their meetings with their Chair in interesting dialogs about the content in place of their own written work.

To counteract the "still reading, not ready to write" syndrome when meeting, the Chair can refrain from engaging in the interesting dialog and switch to interviewing the candidate about what they have learned and what themes they are formulating. By taking notes or recording this interview, the Chair has the fodder to then hand to the candidate, telling them to write down what has just been said, then go back and support it with citation. The blank page is the biggest fear for this procrastinator, and sometimes finding success in small things leads to the willingness to repeat the experience one day at a time until done. Having a routine and creating self-imposed daily writing requirements is something that a Chair can suggest, but that the candidate must have the strength to uphold.

Revision Is Failure

This thesis or dissertation is a mystery to the Chair for months on end. As a perfectionist, the candidate cannot hand a paper in with any possible errors of judgment or format. At the same time, it is typical to be stuck not knowing what pitfalls or errors the Chair will find. Either much is written but not shared, or little is written. It is difficult to get this candidate to admit to the state of the writing; he or she cannot bear looking weak to the Chair.

> ***Case in point:*** *Lee was one of the most efficient and insightful students in the classes leading up to the thesis, but now after one very productive meeting with his chair, he has not contacted Dr. B or returned emails. In fact, when Lee ran into Dr. B at a conference, he tried to leave the room unnoticed. Dr. B invited Lee to have some coffee together, and after a lot of talk about the conference, Lee said that he had most of the reading and several pages of literature review done. Dr. B suggested that they meet to look at the draft and noticed how uncomfortable Lee was and vague about setting a date. Was nothing written, or was there a personality conflict that Dr. B could not see? After several more weeks, Lee responded to another email saying he was not ready to have anyone else read his chapter yet.*

Like Lee, those who will not let the Chair see incomplete work need to find someone who has the expertise who will help. It is tough to rely on others for writing assistance, as the assistance can turn into actual writing. Also, the support system may not have access to the policies or format needed and steer them in the wrong direction. If candidates have various sources of support, with different areas of expertise in research and writing, it is more likely they will get balanced feedback.

One way of getting someone going who is stuck is to open a Google doc or other shared writing form and write "with" them. The Chair does not actually write but offers questions and immediate feedback as the student writes. This, of course, is a short-term solution, offered to let the student know what the Chair is thinking about the subject and the form. Once the student is more confident in knowing how to please the Chair and in having the Chair see drafts, writing usually flows.

Get Along

A candidate who has the primary intent to Get Along in thesis or dissertation writing seeks approval by putting the Chair in the role of judge. Every word and silence is weighed, as the value of the work is measured in the positive and negative feedback. Avoidance of conflict can just postpone facing issues, so this puts initiating action on the Chair's shoulders. Scott's (2017) *Fierce Conversations* describes a confrontation model that both provokes action and strengthens the relationship. The steps are name the issue, provide an example of the problem, clarify what is at stake, identify your contribution to the problem, and invite the other to respond. Then the confrontation should become an interaction that elicits common comprehension through paraphrasing and perception checking until a stated resolution is found. Those who Get Along collaborate on a shared problem when they do not feel the situation is set up to be a conflict between people.

Broken Record

In the repertoire of those who are extreme Get Along candidates, one way they avoid problems is to tell stories eliciting sympathy, go back and revive old issues, and deflect with many words and sometimes humor or tears. To remain empathetic as a Chair, some listening for the real worries or fears beneath the smokescreen is necessary. Then the Chair should find one succinct message of suggested action.

It is important to prepare a clear message, so it is ready when the chance to speak arises. Interrupt at an appropriate time by saying the person's name and repeating until it they pause. Hearing our names causes us to focus our attention on the speaker for a few seconds. When the focus comes, say, "I understand that (*rephrase their issue succinctly*), and so (*tell your message*)."

Even if the two parts of that sentence do not hang together logically, this tells them that they are being heard and that there is a message for them to hear. As they continue their woes, at intervals consistently interject, "I understand, and (*repeat your message*)." Eventually, they find that the Chair is not wearing down and when they are listening to the message, a calm, factual analysis without blame with a plain plan for the future may diminish future conflict avoidance performances.

Just Tell Me

Combining Get Along and Get It Done intents are candidates who have little patience with working out their own problems. These students answer Chair's questions with, "How am I supposed to know? You're the professor," or "We never covered that in class," or "Would you just tell me what to do?" Sometimes the emotional fatigue of trying to earn a living, raise a family, and write a dissertation puts the strongest student in this place.

If it is an unusual response, it is time to help them over the hurdle. By the Chair suggesting solutions or providing a model, this candidate can move beyond the problem. When it is a typical response, however, it is a sign of someone who is not committing or engaging in the mental tasks a dissertation or thesis takes. "Just telling" this person is not the solution, but the opening for the next cry for help. A copy of a self-help book such as *Dissertation Destination* (Foss & Waters, 2007), *The Portable Dissertation Advisor* (Bryant, 2004), or *The Dissertation Journey* (Roberts, 2010) can give the student suggestions without seeking the Chair's support too often.

Get Appreciated

The candidate who is beyond the Get Appreciated intent engages in attention-getting behaviors. While this can be friendly relationship building, in times of difficulty, the attention seeking can become strident because the student sees himself not valued highly. While all candidates expect immediate, detailed feedback, the Get Appreciated candidate views any delay personally. Telling this person that his or her paper will be read as soon as class is taught, tests checked, and so forth, is interpreted as the student not being as high a priority.

It is good to let all candidates know that their work will not be responded to instantly. Work that takes six weeks to create deserves more than six minutes of review and pondering. What is helpful for Get Appreciation is the immediate reply, "I received and printed your work today. Your efforts through this portion are moving you ahead. If you do not get your feedback in one week, please call to check on delivery. I am looking forward to reading your thoughts!"

Some Get Appreciated students call too often, visit too long, ask unneeded questions, and even bring gifts to keep the Chair's focus. Setting boundaries with what constitutes the need for a call or visit and what can be handled through other sources is a start in maintaining a professional distance.

Save the World

A dissertation worth doing is one that earns a Pulitzer, Nobel, and Academy Award. It should solve one of the world's great problems and prove new theories that are jaw-dropping. Sometimes that glorious vision of a completed dissertation or thesis does not turn itself into action toward a realistic goal. Questions that merely suggest or indicate change, methods that explore or examine possibilities, and conclusions that add just a bit to the knowledge in the field are seen as unworthy.

> **Case in point:** *Geena's expertise in technology and adult learning challenged her to study cutting-edge software and strategies to improve online education. She had access to a large number of participants who admired her knowledge and responded to her survey. With a massive amount of demographic data on her participants, Geena analyzed every variation, every item, and every com-*

bination that she could. She enjoyed creating the tables and all the details she could uncover.

When she tried to interpret the variables, there were so many factors that she was frustrated in getting clear interpretation or conclusions. She wanted to show all her work and resented being told to set aside any analysis that did not directly answer her research question.

When a Get Appreciated like Geena wants to save the world, trouble often manifests when the general topic needs to be narrowed. These students write at length about the need for the study, and the problem statement is a rallying cry. However, strong research means that the practical side must be balanced with vision, and so limiting the study to the candidate's skill and time frame is the task. Using other completed studies to show how the narrow focus adds power to a larger idea can demonstrate the balance.

Keeping the conclusions from being overgeneralized also is ongoing in each chapter. The good news is that at the end of creating a successful thesis or dissertation, the Get Appreciated candidate feels fulfilled in seeing how small things add to the larger picture, and the accepted defense shows the admiration of the faculty for the effort.

Clever, Novel

It is sometimes a misconception of those entering the research phase that what is written must be more intellectual and profound than clear and precise. These Get Appreciated students have often been praised as children for being smart and want to continue to demonstrate their skills in vocabulary or innovation. Like a magician, their reward is the gasps from the audience at their slick, clever reveal. Too often, this desire overshadows the straightforward relating of solid research; they are attracted to the novelty and hope their sleight-of-hand writing techniques distract from any research flaws.

Sometimes these students complain that the library and field work are boring. They are drawn to a flashy topic, then slow down as meticulous work is required. They value cute titles and punch lines. These writers need to develop the balance between their written message craft and their research purpose. Cleverness in writing is like salt in cooking—too little is flat and tasteless, but too much is indigestible. When helping this candidate review a draft, use one color highlighter to mark main ideas, a second for evidence, and a third for literary or imaginative sidelights. This visually shows when the balance is missing without making a judgment.

When someone craves appreciation, praising baby steps in the right direction, pointing out the power in plain speaking, and admiring the effort instead of the clever can help channel stronger work. Rather than crush the person by striking out their cute or off-track work, suggest they put it aside "for now" and use it in chapter 5 or as an appendix. By the time they are at the end of the dissertation, they usually do not resurrect the things set aside, but sometimes they really do have a place at the conclusion that was not appropriate earlier in the paper to create a satisfying end.

LOOK IN THE MIRROR

In thinking about those who Get It Done, Get It Right, Get Along, and Get Attention, as Chairs it is natural to think of our own intent as we respond to stress. When students cannot move forward at some point in the process, as mentors we need to wonder if, as Walt Kelly, "We have met the enemy and he is us." Being aware of our own motivations, worries, and response behaviors can help in becoming more empathetic. Jim Collins (2001) calls this strategy looking in the mirror and looking out the window.

In good times, a great leader looks out the window at all the people and groups around to point out their efforts in making the success. In tough times, great leaders then look in the mirror to see how they may influence others and change themselves to improve the situation. Unsuccessful leaders do the opposite—they look in the mirror to take the credit in successful times and look out the window to see who can be blamed for failures. This fundamental attribution error makes the leader feel better but solves nothing. To see possible avenues for progress, use less of the Golden Rule, "Do unto others as you would have others do unto you," and work from the Platinum Rule, "Treat others as they wish to be treated."

Unfortunately, sometimes the miscommunication, delay, or misunderstanding can be the Chair's fault. Even if the difficulty was unforeseen, unavoidable, or an act of God, the candidate's anger overrides other considerations. Sam Horn's *Tongue Fu!* (2004) advocates when being blamed fairly or unreasonably, respond with AAA—agree, apologize, and act. It is always possible to agree that the situation is stressful, difficult, and a problem. That does not mean that blame is being accepted, but agreeing with an angry person leaves them nothing to argue about. Apologizing means that the Chair is sorry that the situation is happening, which is demonstrating empathy. Acting does not promise to make any change or decision, but that something is going to be thought about, or discussed, or considered. The furious phone call from a candidate who is accusing the Chair of delaying graduation can be told, "It is so disappointing not to graduate as you had hoped (agree), and I am sorry that there was miscommunication about the deadlines (apologize). I will check with the graduate college to see that there will not be any more fees or delays for next semester (act)." This not only calms anger but buys time to try to repair any errors—no matter who caused the situation.

DATA OR TOPIC DILEMMAS

One of the fears in conducting ongoing research is that the data or the topic will become obsolete, redundant, or without significance. It is always a risk that the survey sent out will not be answered, the focus group not show up, the instrument not yield meaningful results, or the field advances in another direction. One way to prevent this in a dissertation or thesis is for the Chair to play devil's advocate when the method and question are being developed. Ask what happens if the expected results do not occur. By planning for less-than-perfect situations, the hypothetical barriers become possible pathways that can be addressed in the proposal setting rather than popping up in data collection.

However, sometimes the barrier to the expected outcome arises during or after the data collection. The candidate is truly frozen at this point and is frightened that the Chair will advocate dumping the topic and starting all over. It is also when the Chair must become, or find, a savior to reinvent the study; their student has read extensively in their field and has expended a good part of life in creating an expertise for themselves. Starting over would be a failure of the committee and the institution that did not do enough at proposal to set the student up for success. Luckily, even a broken clock is right twice a day, and while it can take time and effort by a Chair to find the solution, studies can be tweaked or salvaged from disaster.

> **Case in point:** *Phyllis worked with new refugees and studied the trauma factors that impact their long-term success. Her dissertation gathered information from social workers and educators who worked in a first-year refugee program for a midsized community, to determine which trauma factors changed significantly over the year. When her data was gathered, it was so patchy and incomplete that she could not perform quantitative tests for significance, and the qualitative data was of such varied quantity and focus to resist finding trends. Yet she did have interesting results.*
>
> *Her barriers to getting data included the wide variety of ages, cultural differences, parent trust, philosophies of the care providers, developmental differences, and language issues. These were actually not barriers—they were her findings. In the exploratory work of this field, finding out why we do not know what we want to know is a positive first step. It was hard to get Phyllis to see that she had a successful study in hand; it was not the one for which she planned, but the results were meaningful and could lead to future studies.*

Seasoned researchers know that the data takes them to new and unexpected places, and they have the luxury of not having to worry about a committee or a graduation. Candidates believe that unless they prove causation or create black-and-white conclusions, they are vulnerable, and the role of the Chair is to allay the fear of being too loose or insignificant but create a healthy fear of being too definitive or overgeneralized.

Finally, dissertation and thesis work has policies and procedures attached like training wheels to support novice researchers. It is up to the Chair to decide when the wheels need to come off to create a successful study.

POINTS TO CONSIDER

- Expect a stressful, bumpy process. A good Chair sets a student up for success but cannot and will not prevent unforeseen difficulties.
- Learning each student's predominant style or intent (Get It Done, Get It Right, Get Along, or Get Appreciated) suggests how to motivate the changes in attitude, writing, and pace to reach a satisfying dissertation.
- Be empathetic. When the student is frustrated, remember that it is not all about you—you need to stay away from placing blame and be emotionally detached enough to suggest alternatives and insights. Yet it is all about you insofar as your guidance has lasting impact on the new research and the new researcher.
- When things go well, "look out the window" to credit all who have led to success, and when times are tough, "look in the mirror" to see how you can influence the situation positively.

Chapter Nine

Litigation Around the Dissertation and Thesis Process

CASE STUDY—PART 9

When Chair read Student's latest draft, familiar language and wording not in the style of the student brought forward the idea of plagiarism by Student. When Chair checked the work electronically, there were not large blocks lifted from a single source, but it was evident that Student did not understand, or did not respect, the need for clear boundaries between original and cited work.

In addition, during the course of the past few semesters, Chair began to hear rumblings during faculty meetings about a student who was unable to finish her dissertation for a variety of reasons and was becoming very confrontational with her committee. She began to allege that the committee was treating her unfairly and at one point stated that if she didn't get her degree by the end of the year, she was going to sue everyone in the department for harassment.

Chair knew her own work was ethical and professional, but she began to wonder what her own students would allege if things did not go smoothly or if Student was simply incapable of finishing his paper. Was she in danger of losing her job or worse yet, causing the university to face legal trouble?

- *When issues are first noticed by the Student or the Chair, who else should be in the conversation to protect the rights of all parties?*
- *If the Chair or Student feel that their rights are not being respected, or even if they just feel uncomfortable about what is happening, under what conditions should there be a face-to-face confrontation?*

97

- *How can Chair protect her reputation and professional image when dealing with Student?*

Completing a master's or doctoral degree is not an easy task and often takes several years to complete, if completion, indeed, happens. Unfortunately, the rate of completion for doctoral students across the United States is about 57%. While litigation by students pursuing doctoral degrees is uncommon, it does happen and can be of concern to universities and faculty who deal with doctoral and thesis students. Most frequently, it is the sometimes-poor relationships between the Chairs and students that are the crux for litigation.

Typically, failed dissertations that end up in litigation fall under four categories:

1. student/faculty relationship fallout;
2. student failure to complete within a required timeframe for a variety of reasons;
3. conflicts of ownership and authorship; and
4. plagiarism.

We reviewed published case law from the past few years to inform this chapter and selected cases that we felt would best inform the practice of a thesis or dissertation Chair. What follows is a summary of those cases within each of the four identified themes that emerged from our readings as well as some best practices within each area to help faculty navigate these issues.

STUDENT/FACULTY RELATIONSHIP FALLOUT

The relationship between thesis or doctoral student and Chair can be fruitful, challenging, and productive—sometimes all at the same time. Chairs are charged with overseeing student research, adhering to university policies, and communicating with students about dissertation progress. Graduate students also maintain a burden for communicating with those on campus—and it cannot be emphasized enough that this communication is a two-way street. However, because writing a thesis or dissertation can be extremely stressful and might even prevent a student from progressing professionally, the pressure can lead to unintended behaviors and consequences. The cases reviewed in this section present fact scenarios where communication between student and advisor failed, some because the advisor abused his or her position and others because the student failed to take responsibility for his or her work:

Lee v. Guikema, 645 Fed. Appl, 780 (2016)

Lee was dismissed from her PhD program at Kansas State University after multiple warnings from university officials that if she did not obtain an advisor, she would be terminated from her PhD program. Her initial advisor, Dr. Wang, was the only faculty member whose expertise matched Lee's chosen topic, which involved an area of statistics research that was at that time on the cutting edge. Lee asked that Wang be removed as her advisor, claiming that she was too irresponsible for her advisory duty. The department head gave her four options including to keep working with her present advisor, pursue a new topic, file a grievance, or terminate from the program.

According to the doctoral handbook, students who fail to make satisfactory progress will be terminated from the program. Dr. Neill agreed "to serve as a mediator" between Lee and Dr. Wang so Lee could keep working on her chosen dissertation topic. But despite Neill's intervention, Lee remained dissatisfied with Dr. Wang and filed another grievance.

On April 4, 2012, Lee's grievance was approved, and Dr. Wang was removed as her advisor. Dr. Neill then notified Lee that she was free to find another professor within the department and continue her work, but she needed to keep him informed so he could track her academic progress. Lee contacted all twelve of the remaining statistics faculty members, but none agreed to advise her on the dissertation topic she had selected with Dr. Wang. Still, Lee refused to change her dissertation topic.

Neill told Lee that if she wanted to be considered for a graduate teaching-assistant position, he needed her to find a new advisor. Lee failed to meet the deadline and lost her teaching-assistant position. Lee complained to Dr. Guikema that Dr. Neill had canceled her teaching-assistant position and was "forcing her to select a new PhD research topic." She acknowledged that she was facing termination from the program. In response, Guikema advised Lee to stay focused on obtaining her PhD and noted that because her options for success in the statics department were "nearly zero," he suggested that she "explore discussion with the related graduate program."

In the meantime, KSU's director of student life received a report that Lee had been yelling and disruptive in the graduate school office. Dr. Neill informed the statistics faculty of the report and surmised that Lee would be terminated from the program. Guikema met with Lee and told her that the statistics department would be recommending her dismissal from the KSU graduate program because she had not found a replacement advisor. Guikema offered not to process that recommendation for six weeks so she could pursue graduate opportunities in other departments.

Neill and the graduate student progress committee submitted the termination recommendation based upon Lee's failure to find a replacement major professor to supervise her PhD research. Lee had not sought admission to any other department at KSU, and she notified the graduate school that she had decided not to transfer. The next day, Lee was dismissed from the graduate program. After unsuccessfully seeking reinstatement, Lee sued KSU, Dr. Wang, and various school administrators. The district court dismissed all of Lee's claims except her procedural due process claim against Drs. Guikema and Neill. The district court applied qualified immunity and granted summary judgment. The Court of Appeals judge held that the student's dismissal from the program did not violate procedural due process.

Jenkins v. the Univ. of Minnesota, 131 F.Supp.3d 860 (2015)

Jenkins entered the University of Minnesota in the fall of 2011 to pursue a PhD in natural resources and science management. The summer before she began her studies, she was offered a prestigious work opportunity as a researcher collecting data on peregrine falcons on the Colville River in Alaska. The project was collaboration between several research entities and was aligned with her exact academic interests. Swem, a scientist from the U.S. Fish and Wildlife Service and a leading authority on the falcons, was stationed in Fairbanks, Alaska. Swem's role in the project was to be a mentor and guide, teaching Jenkins how to collect and sort data, as well as how to survive in the remote region.

In June and July of 2011, Jenkins and Swem embarked on two 17-day research trips to the Colville river, and almost immediately, Swem began telling sexually explicit jokes, asking Jenkins personal questions about her dating life, and telling stories of prior sexual encounters and relationships with previous graduate students. He took inappropriate photographs of her and commented on "the scenery." He bathed naked in the river in front of her and encouraged her to do the same, telling her that she was too modest. He also made reference to her needing a "pool boy" to accompany her on research trips.

Between and after the trips, Jenkins stayed in Fairbanks, Alaska, for a couple of weeks to analyze the data. In Fairbanks, between the trips, Swem invited Jenkins on a social outing including offering to take her rappelling and kestrel banding, stating that she would need those skills on her second trip.

On the day of this particular outing, and once they were fairly far outside of Fairbanks, Swem claimed he forgot the rappelling equipment. Instead, they banded kestrels and had dinner together at a restaurant. He offered to be her pool boy and give her a "horse bite" while they were in the car together. When they arrived back at his house later that evening, Jenkins went inside to retrieve her computer. Swem left the lights off in the house and stared at her. Another time, Swem invited Jenkins to lunch under the pretense of discussing logistics of the upcoming trip, even though it quickly became apparent that the trip was already planned.

He complimented her physical appearance and told her he was interested in a romantic relationship with her. He joked that they should bring only one tent for the next trip and that she was welcome in his tent anytime. He also told her that she should just sit in his lap and kiss if she wanted a relationship with him. He acknowledged that his behavior could be construed as sexual harassment because of the power dynamic but suggested that his role could be changed if she was interested in pursuing a relationship.

Jenkins informed Swem that she wished to keep their relationship professional. During the second trip, Dr. Andersen, Jenkins's academic advisor at UM and a collaborator on the research project, was present for the first seven days of the trip. Swem did not tell any sexual jokes or otherwise act inappropriately during that time, but as soon as Andersen left, Swem resumed his aggressive sexual advances.

On one occasion, as they rappelled down to a nest site, Swem described what he thought it would be like to kiss her. Jenkins could not physically distance herself from him at this point, so she did not respond at all. Swem also brought alcohol on the trip and encouraged Jenkins to drink every night. He suggested they celebrate their last night of the trip by finishing an entire bottle of whiskey together, but Jenkins declined. Swem continued to pressure Jenkins on the question of why she wasn't interested in a romantic relationship. She repeated that they worked together and offered several other reasons as well.

When they returned to Fairbanks after the second trip, Swem invited Jenkins to dinner at his house on multiple occasions, always offering her alcohol. She also went there on occasion to shower and to use his laundry facilities, because she did not have running water in her cabin. Swem continued to discuss his desire for a relationship with her, explaining that all the reasons she gave for not dating him were logistical and could be overcome. Jenkins again explained that she had no interest in a romantic relationship with him.

When she arrived back at the University of Minnesota for the beginning of the fall semester, Jenkins learned that she and Swem were assigned to share an office space. He was to be there for one academic year, analyzing his Colville river data, among other duties. Swem continued to invite Jenkins out on social outings, including dinner and hockey games, though he did not make any further sexual comments. Jenkins eventually started doing her graduate work in coffee shops or libraries to avoid Swem. She stated that he was "always" in their shared office with the door closed.

After failing a statistics exam, Jenkins sought counseling. The counselor suggested that she was suffering from anxiety and stress related to the situation with Swem and that she should talk to her advisor about relocating to a new office. On Friday, November 4, 2011, Jenkins discussed Swem's behavior with Dr. Andersen for the first time. Andersen made a new office space available next to Jenkins on the following Monday, but it took some time for internet access to become available, meaning that the new space was not immediately useful.

In January 2012, Jenkins resigned from the University. She had since been diagnosed with PTSD, depression, and anxiety. Jenkins brought suit against UM, Swem, and Andersen, alleging that Swem sexually harassed her and created a hostile work environment. The court concluded that Jenkins's right to be free from sexual harassment by a state actor was clearly established under the Fourteenth Amendment. Swem was not entitled to summary judgment because she told him his conduct was unwelcome, she considered his conduct severe enough to alter her employment terms, and a reasonable person would so consider it, as their geographic isolation and her dependence on him for instruction and survival made his conduct severe and pervasive and she suffered psychological harm.

Dopp v. State Univ. of New York, **29 N.Y.3d 906 (2017)**

Kathy Dopp sought reinstatement at the university's political science PhD program as a student in good standing. The Supreme Court of Albany County dismissed the petition and the student appealed. The student had repeated conflicts with faculty members and was formally referred for disciplinary action based upon her alleged violations of the Student Code of Conduct. A year-long disciplinary suspension was put into place. The board further stated that if the petitioner was readmitted to the political science doctoral program, she would be placed on disciplinary probation through graduation and would be required to meet with appropriate faculty to develop a written agreement with clear behavior expectations.

The faculty were concerned with her lack of progress and requested that she voluntarily withdraw from the program. She refused, and the chair requested her dismissal, citing her inability to respond appropriately to constructive criticism from a dissertation committee and her unwillingness to complete the program as it was designed. The vice provost of graduate studies indicated to the petitioner that she could provide certain assurance relating to her return to the program, and on August 29, 2012, she signed a performance improvement plan. The plan stated that the faculty had five areas of concern regarding her ability to complete her PhD program including that she complete the required year-long research and writing seminar, adapt her scholarly interests to fit the interest and expertise of the program faculty, and form a dissertation committee in accordance. She was also expected to conduct herself professionally in the classroom and in her interactions with faculty and students. If she failed to follow through on the plan, she would be dismissed from the program.

Following another behavioral incident, it was again recommended that she be dismissed from the program. The vice provost contacted Dopp and indicated that there was sufficient cause to act on the political science department's request and move toward dismissal based upon her failure to comply with the plan. She refused to withdraw voluntarily and was expelled. The academic council denied her petition for reinstatement. The record demonstrates that the petitioner's dismissal was based upon the university's academic assessment that the petitioner lacked the ability or effort needed to succeed in its political science doctoral program and, thus, its determination to expel her was not arbitrary or capricious, irrational, made in bad faith, or contrary to constitution or statute.

Best Practices for Thesis and Doctoral Chairs

Responsibility for maintaining a relationship to help a student attain a graduate degree rests on the shoulders of both the student and the faculty member. This relationship is crucial and cannot be underestimated. In nearly all of the cases we reviewed, the problems originated with the breakdown of the faculty-student relationship. While students maintain primary responsibility for making progress, writing chapters, and setting up committee meetings, faculty members who are unresponsive or slow to communicate can stall the process and waste time. In addition, personality differences can cause stress and strain during the years-long course of a doctoral relationship. In order to better manage this relationship, we suggest the following:

- Always communicate in a timely fashion with students, even if it means "I'll get back to you later" when responding to an email. Never let a student sit and fret wondering what your response will be.
- Consider the student's feelings when critiquing a student's work. While we may not intend our advice to be a personal attack, the student may hear it in a different voice and may take the criticism personally. Be clear about the purposes of your critiques and what a student should do to implement changes.
- Document your interactions with students. This can be critical should a student become a physical danger, but also if a student becomes confused about what you may have said or done during a certain period of time. We think it is fair to share with the student that you maintain all documentation.
- Maintain and model professionalism. Graduate students are under stress and pressure, some that we know nothing about. It is a faculty member's job to demonstrate how to behave and speak in the academic world. Thus,

while your student may essentially be an intellectual peer, you should treat him or her as a learner who is modeling what you say and do.

- Clarity cannot be understated. Be clear about deadlines, revisions, expectations for citations, when you will read drafts of papers, how much of those papers you will read, how many times you will read a draft, when and where a student can expect feedback, and when and where a student can reach you to communicate.
- Kindness can also not be understated. Graduate students are generally high-achieving, intellectual people who want to do well. While cases may show difficulties between advisors and students, many, many relationships are built on a strong foundation and continue throughout academic careers. Find ways to support and encourage your students, from supportive emails, to informal chats, to learning about personal and family adventures (Oltman & Surface, 2018).

STUDENT FAILURE TO COMPLETE WITHIN A DESIGNATED TIME FRAME

Graduate students generally have several years in which to complete their degree after attaining candidacy status. This time span is usually anywhere between seven and 10 years, depending on the institution and the requirements set forth by that entity. Through the case law reviewed, however, there are several issues that can arise during that time-frame that can cause a student to miss that deadline—personal injury, sickness or illness, and failure to work well with a dissertation advisor. A review of pertinent cases follows.

Vigil v. Regents of the Univ. of Michigan, 980 F. Supp. 2d 790 (2013)

The student failed to complete his doctoral degree within the required six-year time line. During the coursework in his political science PhD program, his failure to produce a solid dissertation draft met the chagrin of several faculty members. The student's topic was never quite clear, and he had failed to disclose where he collected his data after being questioned regarding it. Several committee members, over the course of multiple years, either left the university or refused to work with the student because of the lack of satisfactory progress on his dissertation.

The student eventually exceeded the university's six-year timeframe in which to defend his dissertation and sought relief against the university and the personnel involved with his dissertation. The student raised a variety of claims including a violation of procedural due process. The court found that while the student may have had held a right (which was arguable at best), there was no genuine issue of material fact to show that he had been denied due process in his course of study. In addition, the student failed to produce evidence of any of his claims against the university, including a violation of the First Amendment and substantive due process.

Murphy v. Capella Educ. Co., 589 Fed. Appx. 646 (2014)

Doctoral student Murphy received a bachelor's degree from American University and an MBA from the University of Phoenix. He then sought to obtain a PhD for purposes of his professional development in the business management field. Murphy was impressed with Capella's advertising of their doctoral programs in business management. Capella aggressively responded to Murphy, calling and emailing him and providing with brochures and other marketing materials to enroll him in its doctoral program. He was issued a guide that described the PhD program in Organization and Management, with specialization in Leadership (The Leadership PhD). The guide contained a description of the outcomes of the PhD program along with testimonials and photographs of individuals purporting to be students.

Murphy enrolled in the program because of representations made in the guide, and in the brochures by enrollment counselors. From 2009 to 2011 he performed well and was very involved in school activities. He communicated with his advisors and took classes on a quarterly basis. He attended three residential programs where he met other Capella students.

Through the program, Murphy was in regular contact with his advisors about progress, course selection, and difficulties with his studies. He emailed or called his advisors twice per month. He earned a $5,000 scholarship to apply toward his tuition. He was selected as a Capella Ambassador, and in that capacity, he discussed academic offerings with new and potential students. After finishing his course work, in the fall of 2011, he took the comprehensive examination, which was the last step before a Capella PhD student may begin to write the dissertation.

According to the student's complaint against the university, the comprehensive exams were purportedly written exams that feature multiple essay questions in which the doctoral candidate demonstrates knowledge of the subject matter as well as writing, research, and critical thinking proficiency. If a student fails the comprehensive exam on the first try, he or she may try again, but on the second failed attempt, the student is disenrolled. The comps term was treated as a course, requiring approximately $4,000 in tuition per term. Students were permitted to receive feedback during the process of writing the comps and, in response, perform "rewrites," but this normally lengthened the comps process, adding more to the tuition bill.

Murphy was the author of several books and multiple published articles and expected to pass the writing skill portion. After submitting a draft for feedback, he received negative criticism and exercised his option to rewrite. After completing the rewrite, he was informed that he failed the comps and must take an intervention writing course that cost an additional $4,000. He received an A in the writing course and attempted to take the comps and paid another $4,000.

After being subject to technical and arbitrary criticism, Murphy's essay was flagged for plagiarism, caused by failing to enclose a direct quote in quotation marks. He took the option to rewrite again and was informed that he failed comps for the second time and that he would be "disenrolled." After he appealed, Capella offered him a third opportunity take the exam at an additional cost of $4,000. At this point, he had spent over $70,000 in tuition and elected not to pay the additional $4,000 for what experience had shown him to be a fruitless endeavor.

Murphy did not receive a degree. He indicates that he enrolled based upon false advertising and false statements made by Capella and its representative. He described contacting more than 50 other Capella students, most of whom were pursuing a leadership PhD degree. The students he contacted all stated that they received similar brochures, did not know about the comps require-ment or the overall low rate of passage; enrolled, took classes, and received a high GPA without any indication or warning of deficiency. In addition, sev-eral took the comps and failed them based upon the same issues as Murphy. These other students took remedial classes or sat through retakes of the comps after paying more tuition and finally, became disenrolled without receiving a PhD.

After having paid a minimum of $60,000 in tuition alone, Murphy alleged that Capella awards a minuscule number of doctoral degrees and awards no degree in the Leadership PhD program. He pointed out that Capella adminis-ters the comps in such a way as to maximize the financial yield by requiring every candidate to use at least a second quarter to complete the comps and uses the comps to systematically dismiss doctoral candidates who have com-pleted the course work as a pretext to punitively disenroll students.

The court found that the student candidate did not allege fraud concerning the doctoral program with the required specificity to comply with the Federal Rules of Civil Procedures; specifically, he failed to accurately describe the content of the allegedly false representations regarding the program and failed to describe the time, place, and content of the allegedly false represen-tations or identify the people making such representation or the people re-ceiving them.

Mosby-Nickens v. Howard Univ., **864 F. Supp. 2d 93 (2012)**

A PhD student studying in Howard University's political science department began her course of study in 1997. Per the rules of the institution, students must pass preliminary and comprehensive exams as well as complete an internship and externship prior to beginning dissertation work. Courses that are more than seven years but less than 10 years prior to the final dissertation oral defense are eligible as long as the student makes the courses viable.

The student completed her preliminary exam in 2001, her externship in 2002, her internship in 2003, and upon finishing the internship in 2004 found that her original coursework was no longer valid under the expiration dates of the university. Time began to lapse during the next few years and by 2009 the student elected to take a semester off from school.

At that time, a great deal of her original coursework had expired and had never formally met the "viability" requirement set forth by the program. The student was withdrawn from the program when she failed to register for courses. The student claimed that the university breached a contract with her when it failed to provide her an advisor during the middle of her course of study and that they allowed her to register for dissertation writing courses she was not eligible to take and that she was allowed to continue enrolling even after the seven-year deadline for completion passed.

The court reasoned that the student held the burden of proving that the Graduate School Rules and Regulations constituted a binding contract. In fact, it appeared that the document was intended as a way for the university to share its expectations regarding academic content with the students, not to bind itself to the provisions within. The student failed to present sufficient evidence to prevail on any of her claims, and her case was dismissed.

Every program has vampire students, writes Anne Herbert (2013)—the students who don't grow into their degree work. Their grades are below their peers', they fail a few exams but will not quit. They drag on. They begin work on their dissertation but cannot seem to find a topic and of course it's October 1, and they want to graduate in December. We talk to them about the effort they need to put into writing but the dissertation itself never seems to advance. You talk to them about how they could finish without having a doctorate, and the response comes back, "I can do this." Time passes. The saga continues with no progress.

You realize that as the Chair, you are the one putting in the effort and not the student. Herbert finally sought out a person outside of her department for advice. The colleague exclaimed, "Our university can't afford to have you put that amount of time into one student. You've worked with her on her dissertation, you've offered support that she didn't use, and most people would take her failing her comprehensive exams twice as a sign that it's time to go." Finally, Herbert said, "The guilt of what earlier had seemed to be heartless plotting against a helpless but energy draining foe vanished." What is difficult is the relationship that we form with our students; telling them that they are being dismissed is certainly unnerving. What we need to learn as faculty members is about determining the boundary where faculty responsibility should meet student responsibility and the need to maintain those boundaries.

The relationship between doctoral or master's student and advisor can be fruitful, challenging, and productive—sometimes all at the same time. Graduate student advisors are charged with overseeing student research, adhering to university policies, and communicating with students about dissertation progress. Students also maintain a burden for communicating with those on campus—and it cannot be emphasized enough that this communication is a two-way street. However, because writing a thesis or dissertation can be extremely stressful and might even prevent a student from progressing professionally, the pressure can lead to unintended behaviors and consequences. The cases reviewed in this section present fact scenarios where communication between student and advisor failed, some because the advisor abused his or her position and others because the student failed to take responsibility for his or her work.

Best Practices for Chairs Regarding Time Lines

As evidenced in these cases, following proper procedures and time lines is critical for university personnel. Ensuring that the proper forms are signed by the required deadline, documenting conversations with students, and adhering to published guidelines are critical to maintain a course of consistency for every doctoral student. In addition, it is safe to assume that students are maintaining documentation on the advisor's actions as well—so great care should be taken to save and note any interactions with students. Some suggestions include:

- maintaining a written set of any deviations from mandated time lines;
- preparing documentation of every meeting with a student—including informal—as a means of preserving memory;
- saving emails from the time a student begins a program until at least seven years after a student graduates;
- reviewing university deadlines yearly to ensure that the current catalog is consistent with practices; and
- ensuring that each student is aware of deadlines through publication and access to catalog materials (perhaps put reminders of deadlines along the bottom of forms requiring signatures or schedule a regular mass email to all students describing time lines each semester).

CONFLICTS OF OWNERSHIP AND AUTHORSHIP

Graduate students are engaged in unique research meant to fill a gap in existing literature. Thus, their work is often cutting edge or unexplored. This can be a scary yet exciting adventure for student and advisor alike; however, sometimes the lines of who "owns" what can get muddy. For instance, if the

Chair guides a research project in such specificity that he or she is a partial author, should those rights be attributed to him or her? If a student could not have achieved data collection without the advisor's help, is it a joint venture? Who owns highly prized patents upon graduation? What does a copyright protect of the student's work? This section presents two cases, both of which were unfruitful for the student, yet demonstrate the necessity for boundaries and clear communication about where the actual ownership of research lies (Oltman & Surface, 2018).

Chou v. University of Chicago, 254 F.3d 1347

Joany Chou was a graduate student and later a postdoctoral research assistant for Dr. Roizman at the University of Chicago's Department of Molecular Genetics and Cell Biology. Chou sued Roizman, the university, and patent licensee and assignee, seeking correction of inventorship and alleging fraudulent concealment, breach of fiduciary duty, unjust enrichment, breach of express and implied contract, and academic theft and fraud. The Court of Appeals held, among other things, that:

- the plaintiff was obligated to assign her inventions to the university;
- nonetheless, the plaintiff had standing to sue for correction of inventorship;
- all defendants were properly named as defendants in action to correct the inventorship;
- the plaintiff stated claims against Professor Roizman under Illinois law for fraudulent concealment, breach of fiduciary duty, unjust enrichment, and breach of contract implied in law, but not for breach of express contract or contract implied in fact;
- the plaintiff failed to state claims for unjust enrichment and breach of implied contract against the university; and
- the district court did not abuse its discretion in striking allegations of academic theft and fraud.

Diversey v. Schmidly, 738 F.3d 1196 (2013)

Diversey was a PhD student in the University of New Mexico's linguistics program. During his course of study, he claimed that faculty members did not provide him with the suitable feedback or mentorship that was due to a doctoral student. Upon presenting his dissertation to his dissertation committee, he claimed that the committee never reviewed his final draft. During a series of complaints, a copy of Diversey's dissertation was submitted to the dissertation publication database (ProQuest) against the student's protest.

Eventually, the copy was returned but the student also found copies of his paper in the university library.

The student claimed copyright infringement because his paper had been published without his knowledge; however, he failed to raise the claim within the three-year timeframe necessitated by statute. The university did violate "fair use," however, when it published his dissertation in the university library without his consent. Because this could eventually preclude the student from finishing his dissertation at the same institution or elsewhere, he was justifiably denied the value of a dissertation (this portion was remanded for further consideration).

Nkwuo v. Golden Gate Univ., 2016 U.S. LEXIS 22056 (2016)

Nkwuo was a doctor of business administration student in Golden Gate University School of Business. He failed his mandatory qualifying exam and was dismissed from the program. He claimed that the school failed him because of his differing political beliefs as well as his race and national origin. In addition, he claimed that he was verbally attacked by a professor for being late to class and that after his dismissal from the program, faculty members accessed and used a software program he had developed for his dissertation. Unfortunately for the student, who represented himself in this case, he presented no evidence of fraud or use of the research software by any of his former faculty members and summary judgment was granted to the university.

Best Practices for Chairs Regarding Ownership

A close research relationship between Chair and student is expected as a student charts a course into his or her research. However, clear boundaries need to be established so that the student understands how much of the work done during the dissertation process is "owned" by the student and what might be considered a joint venture between Chair and student. Some best practices include:

- seeking legal counsel from university lawyers for highly scientific or innovative projects, including those that might require copyright approvals or patent issuance;
- clear guidance on how and when a dissertation is considered "published" and who owns what pieces of it;
- clear communication between advisor and student about the nature of "joint" research and how it can be confusing to sort out who owns what;

- perhaps the use of a committee to oversee research developments that could be profitable or commercially marketable in order to mediate differences between researcher and advisor; and
- a regular research forum in which the university shares its expectations for ownership (or lack thereof) with the university community—this might include an informal discussion series, web articles, or advice from the university's legal counsel (Oltman & Surface, 2018).

PLAGIARISM

Plagiarism is becoming a hot topic within the industry of doctoral dissertations. With the advent of plagiarism-checking software and the ability to quickly match terms or phrases through a simple internet search, now, more than ever, it is important for students to properly and fully cite resources used when writing a dissertation. While there are many potential causes for a student to plagiarize (stress, lack of time, not knowing how to cite something, or just plain carelessness), it is the advisor's role to help ensure the integrity of a student's work. The cases presented here illustrate the magnitude of plagiarism and the drastic results of plagiarism on a doctoral student's academic career.

Pfeiffer-Fiala v. Kent State Univ., 2015 Ohio Misc. LEXIS 10967

A doctoral student presented a copy of her dissertation proposal to her committee in 2012. Upon reading the proposal, her committee members had grave reservations about her ability to conduct research, much based on the fact that portions of her dissertation were plagiarized and uncited. The committee met with the student and eventually referred her to the Academic Hearing Panel, where she was found to have violated a student cheating and plagiarism policy. Upon recommendation of her dissertation committee, the student was dismissed from the university.

The student, upon bringing her case against the university for breach of contract, alleged that dissertation "drafts" are subject to editing and revision and that it was standard practice for students to go back and add citations later. However, upon looking at the manner in which the Academic Hearing Panel assessed the plagiarism, its analysis system was not arbitrary or capricious, and it was reasonable that the academic judgment of the committee could be supported.

Jaber v. Wayne State Univ., 487 Fed. Appx. 995 (2012)

A doctoral student's degree was revoked after the issuing university suspected plagiarism within her dissertation and compared it to published sources using a plagiarism-detection software. It was determined that the student plagiarized at least two dozen passages in her dissertation. The student was presented with two options: a formal proceeding with a hearing panel or an informal conference with the dean.

The student was advised that choosing the informal process would forfeit her right of appeal of any decision. She chose the informal process, which eventually resulted in the receipt of a letter of revocation of her degree.

While this one incident was ethically questionable, the university also had documented history of the student submitting a false teacher certification exam score and stating that she had passed exams that she had not. The court determined that the student had adequate notice and choice of the type of hearing or conference she could choose after being notified of the allegations and she chose the informal method. While the university had never revoked a doctoral degree before, university officials noted that there is a first time for everything, including the revocation of a degree (p. 997).

Best Practices for Chairs Regarding Plagiarism

The necessity of original writing rests on the shoulders of the student. However, failing to teach students proper citation models can lead to an increased risk of unintentional plagiarized work by student writers. Universities can take several steps to prevent student plagiarism:

- provide live writing assistance through tutors or online software;
- demonstrate how similarity-detecting software like TurnItIn or Grammarly assesses a student's piece of writing;
- teach writing as a specific class and include discussions on ethics, plagiarism, and authenticity of work;
- provide clear guidelines for what a "draft" can and should contain. Include information about what constitutes an unacceptable level or threshold of uncited works;
- define what a "final" draft is and what can happen if a student submits work that is not original at that stage; and
- provide remediation to students who demonstrate challenges with plagiarism but do so after clearly notifying the student of an academic misconduct allegation and the necessity of learning the content in order to protect his or her status in a program (Oltman & Surface, 2018).

POINTS TO CONSIDER

- On the front end, admit students to the program very carefully. Do they have the capacity to do graduate work at this level? Do they have the drive to complete a thesis or dissertation? Are there any red flags in their academic records?

- Carefully choose or assign a Chair who does not have a personality conflict with the student. A Chair should have expertise in the student's plan for methodology.
- Ensure that expectations for student performance on examinations for candidacy, as well as written and oral exams are clear.
- Determine reasonable time lines for completion of work, especially milestone achievements such as exams, proposals, and defense.
- Review student progress regularly.
- Develop a departmental policy for mediating student-faculty conflicts over dissertation proposals and defenses. Consider using another faculty member or a faculty member outside the institution if necessary.
- Create a policy concerning how many times a student make retake an examination or defend a dissertation proposal or defense. Enforce this consistently and fairly.
- Allow students who are struggling with personal or medical problems to take a leave and file the appropriate institutional paperwork. Ensure that they are able to handle the stress of graduate school prior to returning.
- Enforce time limits. If providing extensions, be sure to note the extension in writing.
- Create a grievance procedure for students that provides a meaningful review of student complaints rather than permitting the grievance committee to always side with the faculty member.
- Train students and faculty on the ethics of discipline and enforce ethical requirements for both students and faculty (Lee, 2014).

Chapter Ten

Preparing the Student for Defense and Graduation

CASE STUDY—PART 10

The final draft was in shape to be defended when Chair realized that while the jitters and butterflies in the stomach were not as pronounced as when actually defending, being in charge of the event had its own unknown challenges. What if the committee voted to not accept the work based on decisions that had been Chair's? If Student let nerves become overwhelming, would the members think Chair had not prepared well or was lax in requiring quality work? What if, for some reason, Student did not pass?

- *How can the Chair check to see if the student is ready and the norms of defending will be met?*
- *What tools are at the Chair's disposal if the student needs rescuing during the defense?*

Reaching the milestone of a thesis or dissertation defense one usually accomplished after traveling the long, arduous road of drafting, writing, and rewriting. Authors Roberts and Hyatt (2019) describe the defense as

> the opportunity to speak publicly about your research study and to defend it. The final defense is a long-standing tradition in academia. Its major purpose is to demonstrate your ability to advocate for and justify your study, including your research problem, methodology, findings, and conclusions. In most instances, it is an exciting, collegial experience. (p. 183)

   The Chair is ultimately responsible for signaling to the student that the final manuscript is closing in on an appropriate final draft and will soon be ready for a formal defense. The rules for scheduling, conducting, and assessing a thesis or dissertation defense vary by institution, but some general guidelines exist that are applicable to most situations. Preparing the student, handling committee disagreements, leading the defense meeting, and preparing for the steps that take place after the formal defense are all considerations at this stage of the process. It is important to remember that not all students successfully defend their dissertation; however, the Chair can help guide an unsuccessful student through the process in order to promote resiliency and further study by the student.

PREPARING FOR THE DEFENSE MEETING

The thesis or dissertation defense meeting is when the student, Chair, and committee members convene to review the student's research, ask questions of the researcher, and offer professional insights on the student's work. The scheduling and duration of the meeting will vary institution to institution, so it is important to contact the institution for formal procedures and rules that must be followed in order for a defense to take place. In most cases, students will formally apply to the institution, indicating a readiness to defend, and the Chair will sign off on that application. Then a set of processes will take place leading the student to the point of graduation.

   In order to prepare the student for the defense meeting, it is important to recognize and acknowledge that the student is, in fact, ready for the upcoming events. This will include having conducted a thorough review of the student's final draft and study results and talking through the study with the student. If the Chair feels that a student is not ready to defend, it is important to be frank and honest with the student. Granted, this conversation may be contentious and difficult, but the Chair's professional guidance is crucial. It may be that a student defends a final product that was not approved. If that happens, be sure to speak up and share concerns with the committee and student.

   A student who is ready to defend should be ready for the act of the defense—or the questioning and scrutiny that is placed on his or her work. Help prepare the student by fostering a collegial relationship during the drafting process where the Chair can question how and why the student is making research choices, writing decisions, or overall study determinations. Talk through with the student about how these ongoing questions are preparation for the defense meeting—that thinking through the answers beforehand will often lead to a more relaxed and confident defense. Try to also read through the student's formal presentation materials and offer advice on length, flow, and content. The more the student prepares beforehand, the more likely the meeting will go well.

Last, share the typical committee protocol with the student beforehand. Be sure to answer questions such as:

- How long should the student presentation be?
- What presentation format(s) can be used?
- What will the structure of the meeting be like?
- When do committee members ask questions?
- What should the student do if committee members ask irrelevant questions?
- What if the student doesn't know the answer to a committee member's question?
- What professional attire is expected?
- What expectations or norms are present in typical dissertations?

It can also be helpful to share a list of the Chair's expectations of the committee during the dissertation or thesis defense. These expectations might include (a) leading the flow of the meeting, (b) answering any procedural questions about the defense meeting, (c) providing insights into the student's study that may not be readily apparent from the final paper, (d) affirming the appropriate question and answer time for committee members, (e) managing conflicts, and/or (f) collecting a formal committee vote.

A TYPICAL COMMITTEE MEETING

While not all defense meetings are similar or predictable, a typical defense meeting will adhere to the following general format with a variety of times assigned to each of the various pieces of the meeting. Be prepared to take meticulous notes during the meeting; students are often very distracted or unable to stay focused on copious note taking.

- The committee meeting begins with the Chair convening the meeting and sharing a brief introductory welcome.
- Committee members introduce themselves.
- The student begins the formal presentation, generally accompanied by a visual presentation of some sort.
- The Chair of the committee members may interrupt the student during the presentation, but generally this is left for the question-and-answer portion of the meeting. However, some questions are best situated while the student is mid-presentation, and these should be handled in moderation and with care.

- Once the student concludes the formal presentation, the floor is opened for committee members to ask questions. Students should be prepared to answer committee questions with evidence from the study, the research process, or academic knowledge about the topic studied.
- When all questions have been asked and answered, direct the student to leave the room so that the committee can converse in private.
- During the private conversation, discuss the strengths and weaknesses of the student's work. Use any guiding rubrics or university grading tool, if applicable. Collect votes from the committee and determine whether the student has passed the defense.
- If the student passed the defense, welcome the student back into the committee room and offer a warm congratulatory message. Allow the student to ask any follow-up questions about the committee. Be sure to discuss any necessary revisions or edits the student may need to make before final preparation of the manuscript is submitted.
- If the student did not pass, share the results with the student and detail the student's strengths and challenges within the dissertation. Allow the student to ask questions of the committee but be cautious of any emotional reactions from the student. If the student seems to be engaging in conflict or attacks against the committee, dismiss the committee members and converse with the student without the committee members present. Then set a time to follow up with the student to discuss a path moving forward.

The Chair has the latitude to direct the defense meeting, so if a different structure is useful, use best judgment to prepare that setting. Ask the student for any presentation preferences (technology preferences, seating arrangements, availability of a bottle of water during the presentation). The meeting ideally will be collegial and one to celebrate academic success.

HANDLING COMMITTEE QUESTIONS

Leading a thesis or dissertation defense meeting is generally a productive, celebratory event; however, it is important to remember the academic focus of the meeting. Nevertheless, the meeting cannot be led without placing the Chair of the committee as the one in charge of the meeting. This is the student's final presentation of work during the degree program. It may even be the culmination of a student's entire graduate career. Therefore, care should be taken in leading the question and answer portion of the thesis or dissertation defense.

Typically, the floor of a meeting is opened to committee members' questions after the student has formally presented his or her work. Committee members may wish to interrupt the student during the presentation, and while that may be appropriate at times for clarity or understanding, it is also important to protect the flow of information from the student, so as not to allow a committee member to begin attacking or degrading a student's presentation while it is still taking place. As Chair, be cognizant of the student's ability to present and to be able to do so with minimum disruption.

Should a committee member become disruptive, try to mitigate the damage. Sometimes committee members do this because they share an expertise in the content studied; sometimes they seek to embarrass or discredit a student. Professionalism is critical during the defense meeting, by both you and the student.

Not only should your student be prepared to answer difficult questions under pressure, but so, too, should you be prepared to handle a difficult committee member. It is your responsibility to manage this and to mitigate a disruption. If a committee member is speaking out of turn, politely review the structure of the meeting and opportunity for questions after the student's presentation. You may need to redirect the committee member's questions. If the committee member persists in interrupting or attacking the student, step in and either dismiss the student from the situation so that you can talk openly with the committee member without the student present or seek to delay the meeting until the committee member's concerns can be alleviated.

A successful defense usually relies on a majority vote of the committee (check your institution's rules on this to be sure). This means that a committee member can tender a negative or no vote and the student can still pass the defense. This is an important point to share with the student beforehand— that sometimes scholars just do not agree or form a consensus and that is not a career-ending circumstance. Many thesis and dissertation defenses have ended with at least one non-passing vote and the student has still worn the graduation cap and gown.

THE POWER OF "I DON'T KNOW"

As you prepare a student for a thesis or dissertation defense, it is important to equip the student with knowledge about how to handle difficult or complex questions from committee members. Generally, the student is considered the "expert" in the room, and usually this is true; the student has spent numerous hours reading the literature and completing the study. However, some committee members like to challenge students with abstract questions or questions that may not have been considered during the research process.

It is imperative that a student know the response to those questions may simply be, "I don't know," or "that was beyond the scope of my study." The thesis or dissertation, after all, is a narrow study in and of itself. It is not what some imagine will "move the ocean," yet the student should be able to navigate his or her decision-making process, how the research was designed, and why the research did not cover every imaginable possibility for study. Reassure students that not knowing the answer is an acceptable and reasonable way to respond to something that may not have been part of the study or that may be ancillary to the topic at hand. Knowing that there may be a time when there is no answer during a defense can often settle the nerves of the edgy defending student.

THE DECISION

A complete thesis or dissertation may not always be in perfect condition to move on to publication or to send the student to graduation. Roberts and Hyatt (2019) list five potential defense committee outcomes:

1. Pass with no revisions.
2. Pass with minor revisions ("changes that require no substantial rewriting" such as correcting tables, adding more literature or conclusions; p. 186).
3. Pass with major revisions (require a "substantial rewrite"; this might include errors in statistics, an incomplete literature review, or a lack of data; p. 186).
4. Defense to be continued.
5. Fail.

The committee may disagree on the final vote, so it is up to the Chair to carefully consider and weigh the rationale for each vote and to tally the final decision. Again, take copious notes that you can share with the student to help guide revisions or necessary changes. And remember, a "passing" vote does not have to be a unanimous consensus by the committee, so failure to sway a member or two into the majority vote is not a necessary conflict to resolve.

CELEBRATING SUCCESS

If all goes well, a successful defense meeting will end with a congratulatory message welcoming the student into the academy of learners who have graduated from your institution. While the formal meeting may be over, there are most likely some procedural steps that will need to be completed, including application for commencement, incorporating any edits or changes suggested by the committee into the final dissertation draft, submitting copyright information for the manuscript, preparing publication and printing documentation, and finalizing any departmental steps to ensure graduation can take place.

Encourage students to finalize their paper as soon as possible; delays in incorporating committee notes and/or edits can cause students to forget to do so or to misinterpret what the committee asked the student to do. In addition, a quick revision turnaround allows the student to revise the final work with the committee comments still fresh in his or her mind.

Sharing the success of your student can be a meaningful and important life event for both of you. Some institutions have celebratory norms, so be sure to investigate these. These may include a reception for students, a hosted dinner for graduates, or something like a congratulatory note sent from the dean. Be sure to participate in whatever you can. Not only did you invest significant time and effort into a growing scholar; so, too, did the student invest in graduate education. Graduation is a recognition of this shared experience so if you are able, attend graduation and if allowed, participate in the hooding of the student.

ADDRESSING FAILURE

Even when all attempts to mentor and guide a student toward defense have been made, some students do not receive enough passing votes to move on to graduation. Some students simply cannot achieve a paper or defense substantial or creditable enough to pass the final oral defense. Hopefully, this situation is not frequent, but as Chair, it is wise to be prepared for the potential emotional reaction of the student or dissention among committee members. The following steps can help a Chair walk through a failing defense vote:

- Confirm with the committee that the student will not pass the defense. Be sure that the student does not fit under the "pass with major revisions" category, but instead, has not met the requirements of the final degree step. Take careful notes as to why the committee votes the way it does.
- Call the student into the committee meeting and share the result. Some students may be upset, emotional, angry, or sad, while others may already know their work was not adequate. Allow the student to ask questions or share concerns with the committee. If the student is overly emotional or borders on unprofessional, end the meeting and dismiss the committee members.
- When ready to listen, share the committee's concerns and rationale with the student. Investigate the protocols of the institution to determine whether the student is eligible to revise his or her paper and apply for another oral defense.
- If the student is able and chooses to continue work on the study, facilitate the process as necessary. Map out a plan to help the student rework the study, revise the writing, and prepare for the next defense attempt.

- If an unresolvable conflict arises between the student and you, talk to your campus resources (department chair, fellow faculty) to plan a route to step down from the committee in order to allow the student to continue to work with a new Chair.
- It may be that you want to leave the committee because you do not feel the student will ever be ready for defense. Again, reach out to your campus connections to determine how best to leave a committee. No institution should require you to remain on a committee where conflict and disagreement is all that is accomplished.

Some students will never pass the oral defense stage. Try not to take this personally. Rather, use the experience as a means to reflect on what went well and where you have room for growth. You may have some accountability in the process, so own your mistakes and admit to how you would have led the process differently. It will not be pleasant, but it also can be a teachable moment from which to learn valuable information for your future committee work.

PUBLICATION AND SHARED AUTHORSHIP

Encouraging your graduate to publish his or her thesis or dissertation work is an important professional step to help document the study's importance and to help the student establish an academic writing path that may continue for years beyond graduation. Some Chairs demand students include the Chair as an author as thesis or dissertation studies are published. We disagree with this tactic for ethical reasons—while the Chair plays an integral role in the research process, the student is listed as the author of the final manuscript. Therefore, if a writing relationship continues after the defense, we recommend working collaboratively with the student to revise and rewrite the dissertation into a new format in order to earn author placement. A mutual investment in the writing process invites the addition of the Chair (and others) into future publications.

POINTS TO CONSIDER

- Take time to prepare your student for the defense meeting. This includes sharing an agenda as well as some general comments on how you anticipate the flow of the meeting to occur.
- Ask questions throughout the drafting process so that your student is used to being questioned about his or her research and/or the research process. This helps relieve some of the nerves that may arise on defense day.

- A defending student should be confident in answering a committee question with "I do not know" or "That was beyond the scope of my study." Sometimes committee members ask questions that are outside the narrow focus of the study or that a student simply is not prepared to answer. A confident response by the student acknowledging limitations and narrowness of scope is completely acceptable.
- Be willing to lead the meeting. That is, be willing to stop confrontational questions, to step in and help your student answer a question that may be beyond his or her expertise, or to ask committee members to stop talking during inappropriate times.
- Get to know your institution's protocols, including necessary paperwork and timing between when a student can apply to defend and when the defense can take place as well as the time line necessary to graduation. Many institutions require a thesis or dissertation be completed by a certain date prior to graduation in order for internal processes and signatures to be gathered (this can range from six weeks to six months).
- Prepare to invest in celebrating a student's success. Clear your calendar to attend graduation and hooding. Participate in receptions honoring the graduates. Meet the family and friends of your student at graduation events and share your excitement in witnessing the student's growth and progress.

Chapter Eleven

Avoiding Mistakes and Missteps

CASE STUDY—PART 11

Chair sighed in relief at the end of the process. It had not all gone smoothly, but Student was ready to graduate and begin his life as a scholar. All that remained from the long process were a bound copy, happy graduation pictures, a heartfelt thank you from Student, and a research conference where the work would be presented. Looking back, Chair discovered that most of what was needed to mentor Student was common sense and common courtesy, but Chair appreciated the new skills and insights learned that could be applied to the next committee. In fact, as Chair reflected on her work with Student, she realized there were some mistakes and missteps she'd hope to avoid making on her next committee assignment.

- *What common mistakes do Chairs make?*
- *What signs of trouble can be noticed early to prevent significant problems in the future?*

Helping new and experienced thesis or dissertation Chairs enter, navigate, and survive the thesis or dissertation journey alongside a student is a complex undertaking. The process can be challenging, rewarding, and one that strengthens a faculty member's expertise or knowledge in a content area. In addition, it is a contribution to the institution and field of study to shepherd novice researchers through their first study and should not be a responsibility that is taken lightly. The process will not always be a smooth one.

It is unrealistic, therefore, to think that there are not dangers and disagreements in the process. The thesis and dissertation journey is not a direct, linear one. Just when secure and satisfied, another unexpected scenario arises and the Chair has at best an enigma to unravel—and at worst a loss of respect, reputation, or even position. As there is no one right way to chair a thesis or dissertation, there are a myriad of ways to go wrong. The following common mistakes, missteps, and blunders common to the Chair position are shared in the hopes that introspection now can prevent future faulty decision making and serious consequences.

MISSTEP #1: MAKE EVERYTHING INTO A BATTLE

Instead, don't sweat the small stuff. None of us start as Chairs and willfully want to enter conflict with fellow faculty members or students. However, situations arise when egos come into play or students become so attached to their writing that disagreements can arise. Decide what is really worth fighting about and for. Is it really that important to remove a section of the writing that the student has passionately and legitimately argued for? Can you risk a conflict with committee members during the proposal process knowing the committee relationship could last for years? Take time to reflect on what is important and what is worth standing up for as Chair. It is usually possible to be the autocratic boss in the situation, but use that leverage to foster decisions that matter on major things such as content revisions and less on things like editing or political battles.

MISSTEP #2: REPEAT THE SAME CONFLICT, REPEATEDLY

Instead, address the underlying problem, not the immediate one. If there are repetitive conflicts, there is a problem that is not being confronted in an effective way. Whether the trouble is with a student, peer, or superior, going over the same points and perspectives while standing by policies and convictions is wearing. Deal with problems and conflicts as they arise. Address underlying issues that may be at hand—perhaps a disgruntled student is facing a personal crisis or maybe an unresponsive committee member has a heavy teaching load and is simply overwhelmed. Be prepared to listen. You may not be able to solve every problem, but admitting an issue is present and attempting to deal with it promptly can preserve energy for disagreements or dissention throughout the committee process.

MISSTEP #3: RELY ON YOUR MEMORY

Instead, document communications, concerns, and concepts. Leading a busy work life leads even the most organized person to rely on memory, shortcuts, and unreliable tactics to get things done. In the thesis or dissertation process, this can be a significant problem. Conversations with students about concerns, changes to writing, or overall processes of the committee should be documented whenever possible.

After a phone call or face-to-face conversation, take time to send a follow up email to verify the content of the conversation and to be sure both parties are clear on the conversation's content. Keep all emails. Maintain a file (paper or virtual) of records regarding the student's program and progress. Document conversations with committee members where the student may not have been privy to the information. Communicate concerns in writing whenever possible. Not only will a paper trail help you if any issues arise; the documentation can also be utilized for future committee work or evaluation purposes.

MISSTEP #4: AVOID ISSUES WITH A POCKET VETO

Instead, calmly face issues while they are small. Some Chairs turn to the "pocket veto," or indefinitely delaying voting on the student's work by holding on to the paper without giving feedback, ignoring calls and emails, and missing meetings. Avoiding conflict is not an effective leadership trait in the thesis or dissertation process. While the pocket veto may keep things quiet and conflict under wraps, the likelihood that problems will emerge heightens. The vain hope that the student will go away is usually not the outcome. Now the problem is not only the initial conflict, but also the lack of communication.

MISSTEP #5: LET THEM GUESS WHEN OR WHETHER THEY WILL GET FEEDBACK

Instead, set ground rules with realistic time lines. One of the most common complaints among thesis and dissertation students is the lack of specific feedback provided on drafts of a thesis or dissertation. Granted, this can be an extremely time-consuming process, but sometimes students experience a gradual reduction of feedback over time. That is, a lot of feedback is provided on early drafts, while later drafts go partially unread or untouched by the Chair. Some of this is normal; once a section is complete, a Chair need not read the work repetitively, but there does need to be an equal amount of attention paid to the student over time, lest the student think you simply are not paying attention or reading the work any longer, especially prior to the defense.

Be clear on how and why you will provide feedback. Find a style that works for you and share your method with the student. If the student has concerns about the frequency or type of feedback, listen. Try to find a middle ground so that both of you are managing a reasonable workload allowing for plenty of feedback.

MISSTEP #6: BE RELUCTANT TO SAY NO TO A STUDENT

Instead, say "YES, WHEN . . ." Graduate students get to higher education by learning how to make the system work for them, and sometimes they seek to cut corners. Some of the best advice given to a new department chair was, "You are about to work with some of the most wonderful and brightest people. They each think they are the exception to the rule." That is true for the Chair-student relationship as well.

Stretching a deadline, ignoring a procedure, or allowing exceptions of any kind opens the door to asking for another concession to follow. It is hard to say no to a student, but the kindest thing is to be consistent and reliable. Moving deadlines is usually prolonging the agony. Ignoring procedures means a precedent has been set. Exceptions are just that—exceptional and rare. If the request is outrageous, a polite refusal with the attached policy or previous email on the topic is enough. If the request is sensible and needed, agree to a narrow interpretation that cannot be widely used by others.

In most cases, it is not necessary to say no. Instead, agree to what they want when the conditions are met. For example, "Yes, we can set a defense date when the final draft has been read and revisions made," works toward the goal better than, "No, I do not set a defense date without knowing whether you will complete the final draft in time or not." *Tongue Fu!* (Horn, 2004) teaches this technique along with other ways to say what you mean clearly and respectfully.

MISSTEP #7: BE THE GRAMMAR SHERIFF

Instead, provide resources until the rules are internalized. One of the frequent causes of disappointment in the thesis or dissertation relationship is the misguided expectations of who does what in terms of editing a student's work. Some faculty are staunchly against line editing and leave issues like grammar, spelling, and organization completely in the hands of the student. While this protects the Chair's time, it can also mean a poor-quality paper at the time of defense. On the other hand, Chairs who invest in line-by-line editing often find themselves overwhelmed in the menial tasks of adding commas and alerting students to spelling errors.

There is no one right way to decide where you fall on the spectrum of how much editing you are willing or capable of doing in a student's work, but there are several considerations to think about. First, after line-by-line editing a student's paper, is the substance of the paper still the student's and the student's alone? Second, are you enabling a poor writer by correcting his or her mistakes? Third, are you a capable enough writer to edit someone's paper properly? If you find a negative answer to any of these, you may want to seek some help. Some institutions allow students to employ professional editing services while others provide such services on campus. Be clear with the student as to how much or how little you will edit the paper. The less ambiguity in this situation, the more ownership each party can have in the writing relationship.

MISSTEP #8. USE JARGON, VAGUE TERMS, SARCASM, AND CONFLICTING DIRECTIONS SO STUDENTS HAVE TO REWRITE AND REVISE REPEATEDLY

Instead, use a consistent language and check for understanding immediately. It is frustrating to the Chair who gets the third draft of disorganized, unformatted, and redundant writing to read again. Often, novice academic writers tend to write in one of two ways: (1) informally, so much so that the paper is conversational in tone and lacks professionalism or (2) overly scholarly (think "thesaurus overuse") in a failed attempt to appear to be knowledgeable. Additionally, students who have been working within a specific discipline field may become accustomed to the jargon and informal language used by experts in the field.

It is vital that students learn to write clearly, in simple yet professional language that can be understood by the average reader. There are typically three messages used when writing: what the writer means to say, what the reader understands, and what the reader thinks the writer meant. Each position is important and should be considered by the thesis or dissertation author. That is, what is clear to the writer may not be clear to the reader, what the reader understands may not be what the writer intended, and what the reader guesses the writer meant is, in fact, not what the writer was seeking to accomplish.

Sometimes this is called the "Grandma Rule"—that is, advise the student to write the thesis or dissertation in a way that his or her grandma (or any other family member not entrenched in the graduate field) can understand. Provide specific feedback to the student on these issues so that the student is clear where language is being used ineffectively or misconstrued. It is frustrating to be the student who is trying to please the Chair and is not able to figure out from feedback what should be done to earn approval.

MISSTEP #9: IGNORE PROBLEMS

Instead, maintain the integrity of your position. From time to time we have worked with some extremely capable, yet stubborn students. These are students who want to bypass the Institutional Review Board, want to use data collected prior to approval, want to submit messy drafts, and want you to ignore the holes in their study. Some of these students become argumentative and angry. Realize that graduate students are no different from any other people—and they are likely to have emotional responses to criticism of the work into which they are investing so much of their lives.

Hard work on the student's part is important, but you are still the Chair. You have the final say on how the paper will look, read, and flow. If you are uncomfortable with something a student has approached you with, say no. Stand firm. Do not let ethical decisions go unnoticed. That does not mean you have to reign over the student, but you do need to lead, and sometimes that can be a really uncomfortable place to be when we are working with students for a long period. Seek help from other faculty or colleagues. Stand firm in what you believe. A student may disagree with you temporarily, but if you demonstrate that you are a fair, ethical scholar, the disappointment will fade to appreciation.

MISSTEP #10: TALK DOWN OTHER FACULTY MEMBERS

Instead, be loyal to the absent. Working with and among other academics can be a rewarding and challenging position. Whether you are working full-time in a faculty role or are only chairing the thesis or dissertation process, maintaining a positive, professional relationship with your colleagues and peers is of paramount importance. Often, students will share frustrations about other faculty members or will say things like "that's not what Dr. Y told me to do" or "Dr. J said you don't know what you are talking about."

Stay cool. Think about how you would want others to talk about you when you are not around. Admit that scholars agree to disagree at times and that overall, rigorous discourse and reflection is what makes academia a rich field in which to work. Accept that you will not get along with all of your colleagues but maintain a professional tone and stance when talking to students.

Refrain from gossip or innuendo. Stephen Covey (1990) notes that being loyal to the absent makes you a more effective leader. If you indulge in airing internal disagreements to students, disparaging those who malign you, or pointing out the fallacies of others, the students will wonder what you are saying about them behind their backs. While it feels good to vent or rebut, it is healthier to think of the consequences and be the person you wish others to be.

In rare instances, the problem is not the colleague, but a third party trying to stir up trouble. Whether it is a student trying to play one against another or a faculty member engaging in power plays, when receiving "He said . . ." or "She said this about you" rumors, speak face-to-face with the person. If the message is being manipulated, a lot of grief is avoided. If there is truly trouble going on, you have shown yourself assertive and honest enough to deal directly and not continue the dysfunctional cycle.

MISSTEP #11: TAKE ADVANTAGE OF STUDENTS AND JUNIOR FACULTY

Instead, practice servant leadership. One great part about working with thesis and dissertation committees is the ability to bring faculty and scholars from different disciplines or fields into the same conversation. Rank, however, may be an issue. Sometimes experienced or tenured faculty members have the opportunity to exploit the status of students or junior faculty members. This sometimes arises when the senior faculty member refuses to edit a student's work (assuming the junior faculty member will take care of it), provides minimal feedback to the student (after all, the student should be honored to work with a tenured scholar), or ignores some of the minute issues that arise (there are staff personnel to take care of signature pages and saving files). Serving as a Chair is just that—a role of service. That is, you should enter the committee work with the mindset to teach and enrich the process for the student. This does not mean doing unnecessary work, but rather being open and available to truly invest in the process.

MISSTEP #12: BECOME TOO FRIENDLY OR TOO CLOSE TO THE STUDENT

Instead, keep professional and clear in all actions and communications. It may go without saying, but there is an inherent power differential between Chair and student that must be carefully monitored. You will spend a lot of time with the student and over time, you will probably get to know each other pretty well. That being said, it is paramount that a professional relationship be maintained. This means clearly defining boundaries as to where and when you will meet with the student, how you will handle personal gifts (those common at holidays and just generally found between friendly relationships), and when you will clarify a boundary-challenging situation to the student.

It is wonderful if you and your student get along well; after all, a rich, mutual learning experience is what we seek through these academic adventures, but it is also important to protect your reputation and that of the student. If you find yourself in an inappropriate situation with the student or if you find personal feelings emerge, it may be wise to seek the counsel of a fellow academic or committee member.

MISSTEP #13: ASSUME THE UNIVERSITY WILL COVER YOU, SO DON'T WATCH YOUR BACK

Instead, be proactive and document your words and actions. If you've read the earlier parts of this book, particularly the legal section, you are aware that the relationship between a Chair and student is often what leads to the success or demise of a student's progress in graduate school. That being said, there are also ethical issues that must be considered, and one of those is how to protect yourself and your reputation in a situation when it might just be you and the student. Because many graduate students work full-time and often need to meet outside of traditional office hours, be prepared for this situation.

Have a regular public place in which to work where you can document your encounters with students and have conversations in public settings. If a student arrives unexpectedly at your home or office, keep the doors open or step out of the privacy and into a public location. If you are uncomfortable with how a student has approached you, speak up. Tell the student you are busy and need to meet at another time. Your safety should be a priority; included in that is protecting your reputation and ethical boundaries that may be challenged.

MISSTEP #14: PRETEND THAT YOU DO NOT MAKE MISTAKES

Instead, agree, apologize, act. The AAA strategy of agree, apologize, and act (Horn, 2004) works equally well when a true mistake has been made as when being accused of a mistake that is not your fault. When people call or come into the office angry, they want to be heard and understood, and they have no time for explanations. If you answer their complaint with a reasonable explanation of why the problem happened, it is interpreted as resistance rather than help.

A sample situation is a student who did not submit the application for graduation by the posted deadline, and now has a hefty fee to pay for late application. The conversation starts with "Nobody told me," and "You should take care of this; it's not my fault." While natural to point out the online reminders, emails, and verbal prompts you and the university provided, the goal now is not to defend, but to deescalate the situation.

Agree first. Note that there are a lot of processes to complete at the end of the degree, and it is frustrating to be told there is an extra fee. It is hard to start an argument with someone who is agreeing with you. The step of apologizing takes finesse to be sorry without taking responsibility. In the sample, it could be, "I am so sorry you are having this extra stress on top of defense preparation," or "I am sorry that this was not completed early in the semester." Hearing an apology lets the person know there is empathy and the message is being heard.

Finally, the act phase is promising only what the Chair, department, or university can do. "I will check with Graduate Studies to see if there are any alternatives," is an action that will not mean that the resolution is not the Chair's responsibility. Sometimes, "Thank you for bringing this to my attention, and I will think about it in the future," is all the Chair can promise or the validation the student wants.

STEPS IN THE RIGHT DIRECTION

Avoiding missteps is a matter of being vigilant in ethics, efficiency, and effectiveness. There is a balancing act that becomes second nature. The balance is between being kind to the student and adhering to policy, between creating a quality study and one that moves swiftly to graduation, and between prioritizing Chair responsibilities and building positive relationships. Experience as a Chair makes the balance easier and preparing students well during their classes for the thesis or dissertation minimizes reliance on the Chair's knowledge. Getting the faculty to work as a team with candidates is ideal but not always feasible. Creating supportive committees limits conflict and shares responsibilities.

Mistakes are inevitable, so it is important to prevent them when it is possible, but to have strategies fix them with minimal stress. When a Chair has multiple students, mixing up candidates' studies means they get the wrong advice. Documenting can help jog the memory and keep promises. Assuming that students understand the jargon and systems that are routine for the Chair but brand new to the novice results in misinterpretations and wasted efforts. Creating a template, outline, graphic, to-do list, or set of definitions or directions can make the common rough places smoother. Then having the student explain the next steps to check for understanding maximizes the chances that things will be right the first time.

Mistakes by the student also become the Chair's work to untangle. It would be nice if all errors could be prevented by clear communication, but it is also true that most students check with their peers or make their own conclusions rather than checking first with the Chair. So, when the unexpected mess lands on the Chair's desk, the first step is to avoid blaming and assigning credit. That can be done later when reflecting how to avoid future messes.

The first action is not to "satisfice" or do the first thing available to make it go away. The first decisions are to uncover the best possible solution available, to involve all needed individuals and offices, and to be an advocate for your candidate. Calm, caring, and controlled problem solving usually works. When it does not, and the student cannot be helped out of the mess, pointing out that he or she is getting the best deal available, and that things could be worse, pushes toward acceptance.

When the day comes that friends gather to honor your long, productive career as you become emeritus faculty, may they not smilingly clap you on the back in order to firmly push you out the door. Chairs who use the position to demand deference, cling to outdated traditions, create petty power plays, turn defenses into know-it-all debates, or make students jump through hoops just because they can, are left with hollow victories and insincere gratitude. Students, peers, and departments need Chairs to be stepping stones rather than stumbling blocks.

At your retirement, may your friends not gnash their teeth and wring their hands because you are leaving them in the lurch as to how to move forward without you. Dumping half-finished dissertations and theses on your peers is a disservice to student and faculty alike. Closely guarding the routes to success, the tips and tricks, that you have garnered means that the effort dies with your exit. Being indispensable now without playing with the team leaves the Chair with no legacy.

Instead, when your career is fulfilled, may your friends raise their glasses in thanks for all you have given and will leave behind. Be the Chair who learns as much as you teach in each study, who is a model of how to conduct research and collaborate productively, and who has contributed to a positive culture that attracts excellence. May you live, love, and leave a legacy so that when alumni and administrators (as well as peers and partners) think of you, they have fond memories and great stories to share. Give them the tools so that when they face a problem, they try to emulate your ways, and when they find successes, they remember how you were the keystone that led them there.

Let your light so shine that they may see your good works . . .

—Matthew 5:16

POINTS TO CONSIDER

- Handle any problems as soon as possible, as calmly as possible, and as kindly as possible.

- Look down the road. Remember that the first way out of the conflict is often not the best, so take a deep breath and take the time to imagine the results not only of the current issues, but future ones as well. Take time before drafting responses to irritated students or colleagues.
- The defense is a stressful time for the student. Reassure the student that he or she is the expert in the room and is probably the most well-read on the topic. Find ways to build student confidence by pointing out study strengths, by maintaining a calm demeanor, and by assuring the student that your support is based on your confidence in his or her work.
- Documentation is important for the student to have to keep on track and for the Chair to have a paper trail. That is, keep copies of drafts, forms, and notes from meetings. After the process is complete and the student has graduated, purge your files and keep only the essentials.
- Follow the Platinum Rule: Do unto others as they would have you do unto them. It is easy for faculty to remember personal issues and conflicts with the student or fellow committee member and handle problems in the same way the problems were handled in the past. Look for new opportunities to build relationships, forge alliances, and demonstrate grace and forgiveness.

References

Abrams, A. (2018, June 20). Yes, Imposter Syndrome is real. Here's how to deal with it. *Time*. Retrieved from time.com/5312483/how-to-deal-with-impostor-syndrome

Amanchukwu, R. N., Stanley, G. J., & Ololube, N. W. (2015). A review of leadership theories, principles and styles and their relevance to educational management. *Management 5,* 6–14. doi:10.5923/j.mm.20150501.02

American Psychological Association. (2010). *Publication Manual of the American Psychological Association* (6th ed.). Washington, DC: Author.

Brinkman, R., & Kirschner, R. (2012). *Dealing with people you can't stand: How to bring out the best in people at their worst* (3rd ed.). New York, NY: McGraw-Hill.

Bryant, M. (2004). *The portable dissertation advisor*. Thousand Oaks, CA: Corwin Press.

Burton, S., & Steane, P. (2004). *Surviving your thesis*. New York, NY: Routledge.

Caffarella, R. S., & Barnett, B. G. (2000). Teaching doctoral students to become scholarly writers: The importance of giving and receiving critiques. *Studies in Higher Education, 25*(1), 39–52. doi:10.1080/030750700116000

Chou v. Univ. of Chicago, 254 F.3d. 1347 (2001).

Collins, J. (2001). *Good to great: Why some companies make the leap—and others don't*. New York, NY: Collins.

Costa, A. I., & Garmston, R. J. (2016). *Cognitive coaching: Developing self-directed leaders and learners*. Lanham, MD: Rowman & Littlefield.

Covey, S. (1990). *The 7 habits of highly effective people: Powerful lessons in personal change*. New York, NY: Fireside.

Creswell, J. (2015). *Educational research: Planning, conducting and evaluating quantitative and qualitative research* (5th ed.). Boston, MA: Pearson.

Diversey v. Schmidly, 738 F.3d 1196 (2013).

Dopp v. State Univ. of New York, 29 N.Y.3d 906 (2017).

Ernest Hemingway quotes. (n.d.). Retrieved November 26, 2018, from https://www.goodreads.com/quotes/5386-my-aim-is-to-put-down-on-paper-what-

Flaherty, C. (2018, March 6). The mental health crisis of graduate students. *Inside Higher Ed*. Retrieved from http://www.insidehighered.com/news/2018/03/06/new-study-says-graduate-students-mental-health-crisis

Foss, S., & Waters, W. (2007). *Destination dissertation: A traveler's guide to a done dissertation*. Lanham, MD: Rowman & Littlefield.

Friedman, Z. (2018, June). Student loan debt statistics in 2018: A $1.5 trillion crisis. *Forbes*. Retrieved from https://www.forbes.com/sites/zackfriedman/2018/06/13/student-loan-debt-statistics-2018/#5cfc12f57310

Goodson, P. (2013). *Becoming an academic writer: 50 exercises for paced, productive, and powerful writing.* Thousand Oaks, CA: Sage.

Grenny, J., Patterson, K., Maxfield, D., McMillan, R., & Switzler, A. (2013). *Influencer: The new science of leading change* (2nd ed.). New York, NY: McGraw-Hill.

Herbert, A. (2013, May 08). The case of the vampire student. *Chronicle of Higher Education.* Retrieved from https://www.chronicle.com/article/The-Case-of-the-Vampire/139099

Hersey, P., Blanchard, K. H., & Johnson, D. F. (2013). *Management of organizational behavior: Leading human resources* (10th ed.). Upper Saddle River, NJ: Prentice-Hall.

Horn, S. (2004). *Tongue Fu! at school: 30 ways to get along better with teachers, principals, students, and parents.* Lanham, MD: Taylor Trade.

Jenkins v. Univ. of Minnesota, 131 F.Supp.3d 860 (2015).

Johnson, D. H., & Johnson, F. P. (2016). *Joining together: Group theory and group skills.* (12th ed.). Upper Saddle River, NJ: Pearson.

Johnson, M. (2012, August 14). The lonely life of the academic [Blog post]. Retrieved from https://www.insidehighered.com/blogs/gradhacker/lonely-life-academic

Krathwohl, D. R., & Smithe, N. L. (2005). *How to prepare a dissertation proposal: Suggestions for students in education and the social and behavioral sciences.* Syracuse, NY: Syracuse University.

Lee, B. A. (2014). Student-faculty academic conflicts: Emerging legal theories and judicial review. *Mississippi Law Journal, 84*(837).

Miller, A. B. (2009). *Finish your dissertation once and for all! How to overcome psychological barriers, get results, and move on with your life.* Washington, DC: American Psychological Association.

Miller, J. G. (2012). *QBQ! The question behind the question: Practicing personal accountability at work and in life.* New York, NY: Putnam.

Mosby-Nickens v. Howard Univ., 864 F. Supp. 2d 93 (2012).

Murphy v. Capella Educ. Co., 589 Fed. Appx. 646 (2014).

National Science Foundation (2018, April 3). *Number of doctorates awarded by US institutions in 2016 close to all-time high.* Retrieved from https://www.nsf.gov/news/news_summ.jsp?cntn_id=244922

Nkwuo v. Golden Gate Univ., 2016 U.S. LEXIS 22056 (2016).

Okahana, H. (2018, April 9). Pressing issue: Mental wellness of graduate students. *Council of Graduate Schools.* Retrieved from https://cgsnet.org/pressing-issue-mental-wellness-graduate-students-0

Oltman, G. & Surface, J. (2018). Dissertations gone wrong 2.0: Legal and educational issues faced in dissertation completion, presented at the Education Law Association Annual Conference, Cleveland, OH.

Patterson, K., Grenny, J., McMillan, R., & Switzler, A. (2012). *Crucial conversations: Tools for talking when stakes are high.* New York, NY: McGraw-Hill.

Riebl, S. K., & Davy, B. M. (2013). The hydration equation: Update on water balance and cognitive performance [Abstract]. *American College of Sports Medicine: Health and Fitness Journal, 17*(6), 21–28.

Roberts, C. (2010). *The dissertation journey: A practical and comprehensive guide to planning, writing, and defending your dissertation* (2nd ed.). Thousand Oaks, CA: Corwin Press.

Roberts, C., & Hyatt, L. (2019). *The dissertation journey: A practical and comprehensive guide to planning, writing, and defending your dissertation* (3rd ed.). Thousand Oaks, CA: Corwin Press.

Savin-Baden, M., & Major, C. H. (2012). *Qualitative research: The essential guide to theory and practice.* New York, NY: Routledge.

Schein, E. (2017). *Organizational culture and leadership* (5th ed.). Hoboken, NJ: Wiley & Sons.

Schlarb, A. A., Friedrich, A., & Claßen, M. (2017). Sleep problems in university students—An intervention. *Neuropsychiatric disease and treatment.* doi:10.2147/NDT.S142067

Scott, S. (2017). *Fierce conversations: Achieving success at work and in life, one conversation at a time* (rev. ed.). New York, NY: New American Library.

Silvia, P. J. (2007). *How to write a lot: A practical guide to productive academic writing.* Washington, DC: American Psychological Association.

Sinek, S. (2009). *Start with why: How great leaders inspire everyone to take action.* New York, NY: Penguin.

Thomas, K. W., & Kilmann, R. H. (2002). *Thomas-Kilmann conflict mode instrument.* Retrieved from http://www.cpp.com

Truss, L. (2003). *Eats, shoots & leaves: The zero tolerance approach to punctuation.* New York, NY: Gotham.

Tuckman, B. W. (1965). Developmental sequence in small groups. *Psychological Bulletin 63*(6), 384–399. doi:10.1037/h0022100

Index

About the Authors

Gretchen Oltman, JD, PhD, has spent over a decade in education as a high school teacher, university professor, and program administrator. Oltman earned a Bachelor of Arts in English from the University of Nebraska–Lincoln, a Master of Arts in Teaching from the University of Louisville, a Juris Doctorate from the University of Nebraska College of Law, and a PhD in Educational Studies from the University of Nebraska. She is a licensed attorney in the state of Nebraska. Oltman currently serves as an assistant professor in the Interdisciplinary Studies Department and as program director for the Masters and Bachelors Leadership Programs at Creighton University in Omaha, Nebraska. She was awarded the 2010 Dr. Ted Sizer High School Level Dissertation of the Year by the National Association of Secondary School Principals. Her first book, *Violence in Student Writing: A Guide for School Administrators*, was published in 2013. Her second and third coauthored texts, *Law Meets Literature: A Novel Approach for the English Classroom* and *The Themes that Bind Us: Simplifying U.S. Supreme Court Cases for the Social Studies Classroom*, were published by Rowman & Littlefield in 2015 and 2018 respectively.

Jeanne L. Surface, EdD, is an associate professor of educational leadership at the University of Nebraska–Omaha. She is an experienced superintendent and principal in Nebraska and Wyoming. Her teaching areas include Public School Law and Qualitative Research Methods. Jeanne is widely published in the areas of school law, rural education, and social justice.

Kay Keiser is chair of the Educational Leadership Department in the College of Education at the University of Nebraska–Omaha. She served as teacher and administrator in the Omaha Public Schools for 25 years. Research interests center on teacher, administrator, and leader dispositions and their impact upon school climate. She has served as chair or member on over 100 dissertation and thesis committees.